IN MEMORY OF ME

Dec 30, 2011

To Ignatius,
   With gratitude for your
unfailing kindness and
priestly example.

Matt

In Memory of Me

~

A Meditation on The Roman Canon

by
Milton Walsh

IGNATIUS PRESS   SAN FRANCISCO

Cover art:

The Savior. Juan de Juanes
Erich Lessing /Art Resource, N.Y.

Cover design by Riz Boncan Marsella

© 2011 by Ignatius Press, San Francisco
All rights reserved
ISBN 978-1-58617-608-2
Library of Congress Control Number 2011926372
Printed in the United States of America ⊗

DEDICATED TO
HIS HOLINESS

POPE BENEDICT XVI

ON THE OCCASION OF HIS
SIXTIETH ANNIVERSARY
OF PRIESTLY ORDINATION

June 29, 2011

He gave beauty to the feasts,
  and arranged their times throughout the year,
while they praised God's holy name,
  and the sanctuary resounded from early morning.

(Sirach 47:10)

CONTENTS

FOREWORD

Very early on in the *Constitution on the Sacred Liturgy*, the fathers of the Second Vatican Council enunciated an important principle: "But in order that the liturgy may be able to produce its full effects, it is necessary that the faithful come to it with proper dispositions, that their minds should be attuned to their voices, and that they should cooperate with divine grace lest they receive it in vain" (SC 11). "That their minds should be attuned to their voices"—this suggests that "a fully conscious and active participation in liturgical celebrations" (SC 14) demands that we attend carefully to the meaning of the prayers we proclaim. The new English translation of the *Missale Romanum* was undertaken with this goal in mind. The desire for a translation more faithful to the Latin prayers was not an end in itself; its intent is to reveal better the biblical allusions and theological riches to be found in the patrimony of the Roman liturgy.

By its very nature, the Eucharistic celebration is an action, and if we are to appreciate the meaning of the prayers we sing or recite, we would do well to make them the subject of personal meditation apart from the Mass itself. Many of us know from experience that personal Bible study enriches our experience of the Liturgy of the Word and that silent prayer in the presence of the Blessed Sacrament allows us to contemplate at leisure the great mystery we celebrate in the Liturgy of the Eucharist. Similarly, our active participation in the liturgy will be greatly enhanced if we take time to reflect quietly on the texts of the prayers we use. This organic relationship between personal prayer and liturgical life was also advocated by the Second Vatican Council: "The spiritual life, however, is not limited solely to participation in the liturgy. The Christian is indeed called to pray with his brethren, but he must also enter into his chamber to pray to the Father, in secret" (SC 12).

For this reason, it is very timely that a book like *In Memory of Me* should make its appearance as the new translation of the *Missal* is being adopted. The First Eucharistic Prayer holds a privileged place among the texts used in the liturgy: it was composed in the golden age of the Fathers of the Church, and for many centuries it was the only Eucharistic Prayer used in the Latin Rite. It is a prayer that expresses the panorama of salvation history in a unique way, and this book reveals how even one word in it offers a fresh perspective on the paschal mystery. What is most striking in *In Memory of Me* is how strongly scriptural its reflections are. The Roman Canon was written at a time when the Christian Latin vocabulary was being shaped, and this was greatly influenced by Jerome's Latin Vulgate Bible. We live in a time when there are a variety of English translations of the Bible, and this is no doubt a great blessing. However, something is lost: when for centuries there was only one translation (as was true for Catholics with the Douay-Rheims and for Protestants with the King James Bible), certain words or phrases automatically triggered biblical associations. This was true of the Latin prayers used in the liturgy, and even a more accurate translation of those prayers can rarely capture those allusions. This book of reflections reveals those connections and helps us appreciate how profoundly biblical our liturgical prayers are.

In Memory of Me combines liturgical scholarship, theological reflection, and liturgical piety in a way that will deepen your understanding of the Eucharist and nourish your spiritual life. My hope is that this book will also encourage you to keep a copy of the *Roman Missal* next to your Bible and to find in it a wellspring of inspiration. As Saint Irenaeus taught us so long ago, "Our way of thinking is attuned to the Eucharist, and the Eucharist in turn confirms our way of thinking" (CCC 1327 [Saint Irenaeus, *Adv. haeres*. 4, 18, 5: PG 7/1, 1028]).

> —MOST REVEREND J. AUGUSTINE DINOIA, O.P.
> Secretary of the Congregation for Divine
> Worship and the Discipline of the Sacraments

PREFACE

Guidebooks sometimes describe a beautiful church as "a sermon in stone". The image can be reversed: a moving poem or prayer creates a space for contemplation, a spiritual oasis. One of the precious legacies of our Catholic patrimony is the Roman Canon, which has come down to us from the time of Saint Gregory the Great (590–604). It was already a venerable prayer in his day; he made a few changes to it, and some minor alterations were effected in the intervening fourteen centuries, but this *sacrificium laudis*, this sublime sacrifice of praise, has reached us substantially unchanged from the era of the great Fathers of the Church. Like a church building, this prayer was created primarily for an event, the Eucharistic liturgy. But also like a church building, a visit apart from the celebration can provide material for personal reflection, reflection that in turn enriches our participation in the Mass. I hope that the meditations in this book might serve as a guidebook to the Roman Canon, so that its profound theology will deepen our appreciation for the great gift of the Eucharist.

Every kind of prayer, like every style of church, creates its own effect. Think of the solemn splendor of a Byzantine church, the soaring transcendence of a Gothic cathedral, or the joyful exuberance of a Baroque chapel. The architectural form that best conveys the "feel" of the Roman Canon is, not surprisingly, the ancient Roman basilica. Many of these churches are still to be found throughout the Mediterranean world, although the embellishments of later centuries often mask the simple lines of the original buildings. Several of them in Rome are relatively untouched or have been restored to their primitive form. They are somewhat off the beaten path, so few tourists visit them.

When you leave the bustle of the Roman street and enter one of these churches, your initial impression is one of austere serenity. There is a great deal of light, but it is filtered through sheets of alabaster or mica; the atmosphere is coolly refreshing. As your eyes adjust to the subdued luminosity, rows of columns carry your vision to the focal point of the building: a simple stone altar-table several feet above the floor of the nave. This altar is sheltered by a stone canopy surmounted by a cross, above which a gleaming apse-mosaic of the risen Christ and saints adds a touch of vivid color. The harmonious lines and perfect proportions of the architecture create an effect of calm and tranquility. Gradually, you notice that the walls of the church are decorated with frescoes depicting biblical figures and saints. Some you recognize, while others are obscure; whoever they may be, their presence is connected to that simple altar in the sanctuary. You begin to take in more details: the columns may not match, suggesting that they were taken from various older buildings; there are side chapels decorated by artists of different periods; the floor has intricate designs in colored stone. You explore for a while, then sit at the back of the basilica and soak in the harmonious balance of the building as a whole. After a time, you plunge back into the Roman street traffic, refreshed from the time spent in this peaceful haven.

This is the mood of the Roman Canon: the sonorous phrases, the balanced sets of prayers breathe an atmosphere of classical *gravitas*. Some liturgical scholars have developed elegant blueprints of the component prayers that comprise the Canon. Others object: to them, the connections seem artificial, and they find a lack of cohesion in the Roman Canon as it has come down to us. There is something to be said on both sides: like a Roman basilica, the fundamental lines of the Canon are clean and well-proportioned, but the prayer took shape over a long period of time, and the piety of different ages left its mark. The Canon is a house that has been lived in, and it is a little untidy. Which is to say, it is a very human prayer.

Like many of the great artistic and architectural monuments of antiquity, the authorship of the Roman Canon is shrouded in anonymity. Very briefly, what we know is this. Since the first Christians were Jews, it is not surprising that their worship was shaped by the Jewish synagogue service and religious rituals at the family table, especially the annual Passover feast. Our sources for Christian liturgy during the first few centuries are rather scant, for several reasons: there was some flexibility regarding prayers; Christianity was a persecuted religion, so both the shape of worship and the ability to express that worship openly were very limited; the underlying Jewish patterns were adapted in various ways as the Gospel took root in different cultures in the Mediterranean world.

The golden age for the development of public Eucharistic rites was from the fourth to the sixth centuries. This was partly due to the changing fortunes of the Church, which in one generation went from being a persecuted sect to the official religion of the Roman Empire. But this was also the era of the great Fathers of the Church, whose writings helped to shape the public culture of Christianity. Several cities enjoyed prominence by virtue of their association with the Apostles and as theological centers in their own right: initially, Rome, Antioch, and Alexandria; with the end of persecution, the sees of Jerusalem and Constantinople (the capital of the Christian Roman Empire) also grew in importance. There was some cross-fertilization as the rites in these areas took shape: so, for example, pilgrims visiting Jerusalem took part in the Palm Sunday procession there and carried the custom home to distant places. Some interesting affinities appear: there are close ties between the patterns of prayer in Rome and Alexandria, while the liturgy of Antioch influenced worship in Gaul and Spain.

As to the Roman Canon itself, we have no clear antecedents before the fourth century. Saint Ambrose cites the central prayers of the Canon and mentions that prayers of praise and intercession preceded them. The prayer continued to develop somewhat over the next two hundred years, and its form was fixed by the time of Gregory the Great, in the late sixth century. Some traditions suggest that Pope Saint Damasus I (366–384) had a hand in the composition of the text. There is no evidence for this; however, he was the pope who commissioned Saint Jerome to produce a Latin translation of the Bible, and he composed elegant verses to be placed at the tombs of the Roman martyrs, so the association is not surprising. It is thought that Pope Gelasius I (492–496) added the *Mementos* for the living and the dead, together with some saints' names; the ninth-century "Stowe Missal" ascribes the authorship of the Canon to him.

As the Canon took shape during those centuries, its authors steered a course between two other models. Eucharistic Prayers of the East were written as an organic whole; our Eucharistic Prayer IV is modeled on these. Different prayers in their entirety would be used on different occasions, and each Prayer narrated the entire plan of salvation. In Gaul and Spain, the custom was to have a collection of individual prayers, and texts would be chosen from among these for particular celebrations. The approach taken in composing the Roman Canon was to have one set prayer that would be used all the time, but with variable parts that could be changed according to the occasion. We experience something similar in the structure of the Mass itself: the "Ordinary" of the Mass remains the same, while the "Proper" (collects and hymns) vary according to the feast or season. The most prominent changeable part in the Canon is what we call the "Preface": rather than relating the whole sweep of salvation history, each Preface celebrates one facet of it.

Very few alterations were made to the Canon after the time of Gregory the Great, and these will be noted when we look at the individual prayers. But doubtless the most significant development was the custom of praying the Canon quietly. Scholars do not agree on when this took place or why. It may have been due to something as practical as the energy required to chant or proclaim a lengthy prayer in a voice loud enough to be heard in a large church; it may have been that as the Roman Rite came to be celebrated in Gaul, the Eastern tradition of a quiet recitation of the Eucharistic Prayer was adopted; or it may have been that over time the choral singing of the *Sanctus* expanded. Certainly the hushed stillness of the Low Mass or the magnificent compositions of a Mozart or Haydn at a High Mass forcefully expressed the sacredness of this central prayer in the Eucharistic liturgy; but it also meant that for the vast majority of Catholics the venerable basilica of the Roman Canon was closed for many centuries.

Today, we can hear this beautiful prayer again, as the *plebs sancta*, the "holy people", did in the days of Pope Gregory. We do not hear it used often, which is regrettable. Some Catholics, priests and people alike, find it somewhat "foreign": all those strange saints' names! All that talk about sacrifices and heavenly altars! Whatever can all this have to do with the Last Supper? And the answer is: everything.

INTRODUCTION

A Setting for the Pearl of Great Price

One cool spring evening a group of friends gathered for a farewell dinner. Most of the men who reclined at table did not know that it *was* a farewell dinner; on the contrary, they may have thought that the prospects of their little band had never been more promising. Just a few days earlier, their Teacher had triumphantly entered the holy city of Jerusalem, hailed as the Son of David. They did not realize that this enthusiastic welcome probably sealed the Master's fate. It was Passover time, and Jerusalem was thronged with pilgrims from all over the world. The multitude of people and the occasion for their gathering—a celebration of the liberation of the Jews from the yoke of slavery—understandably made the occupying authorities nervous. The Romans especially feared insurrections at this time of year, and, with the help of the Jewish leaders who had to act as a buffer between a stern military regime and a restive population, they acted quickly to thwart any trouble. That very night the leader of this band of Galileans was to be arrested, and he would be brutally executed the next day. That last meal was particularly solemn, but only two men at the table knew what would happen later that evening: the Teacher himself and the trusted friend who had betrayed him.

Around twenty-five years later, the Apostle Paul had occasion to remind his flock in Corinth of what took place at that table in Jerusalem:

> For I received from the Lord what I also delivered to you, that the Lord Jesus on the night when he was betrayed took bread, and when he had given thanks, he broke it, and said, "This is my body which is for you. Do this in remembrance of me." In the same way also the chalice, after supper, saying, "This chalice is the new covenant in my blood. Do this, as often as you drink it, in remembrance of me." (1 Cor 11:23–25)[1]

The Corinthians knew the story very well, of course; they celebrated the Lord's Supper regularly, as Jesus himself had commanded. Paul was reminding them because this, the very meal that was supposed to celebrate their communion with Christ and with one another, had become a source of scandalous dissension within the community.

In just three verses, Saint Paul describes the ritual that has been the central act of Christian worship for two thousand years. This brief narrative, related similarly in the Gospels of Matthew, Mark, and Luke, is our pearl of great price. For centuries, artists, architects, composers, poets, theologians, and saints have sought to express the meaning behind these deceptively simple words, to fashion a setting for this pearl. Prominent among these creations are the Eucharistic Prayers of the East and the West. When we read through these formularies, they may seem initially to be far removed from the simple biblical account of the Last Supper. How-

[1] Biblical citations in this work are taken from the Revised Standard Version, Second Catholic Edition.

ever, they are symphonic renditions of the essential themes in the "Institution Narratives" that describe what Jesus did on the night before he died.

We should recall that the original setting for the pearl of the Last Supper narrative was a Jewish religious meal. Such gatherings included the recitation of various prayers, thanking God for the gift of creation and his work of redemption in Israel's history and asking for the fulfillment of God's plan in the future coming of the Messiah and an age of peace and security. The Passover meal was a particularly solemn occasion for recalling God's intervention in his people's history; by hearing the Passover story, those gathered at table entered into the experience themselves. So, when Jesus and his companions reclined at table, he gave thanks and broke the bread at the beginning of the meal and again gave thanks over the last cup of wine at the meal's end. But this was not simply a matter of grace before and after the meal—the Jewish prayers called to mind the whole sweep of creation and God's saving work and asked God to bestow even greater blessings. So far, there was nothing unusual about what Jesus did.

But when he pronounced those traditional blessings, Jesus did something that *was* extraordinary and, in fact, takes our breath away (or would, if the story were not so familiar to us). When he broke the bread and gave it to his disciples, he told them, "This is my body which is given for you" (Lk 22:19). And when he handed them the cup he said, "This is my blood of the covenant, which is poured out for many" (Mk 14:24). And he instructed them, "Do this in remembrance of me" (Lk 22:19).

As devout Jews, the disciples knew that a sacred meal

connected them with the greatest event of their people's history, the Passover; but by these words our Lord associated forever that Bread and Chalice with the event that was to liberate the whole human race from the power of sin and the curse of death—his own self-offering the next day. The Apostles did not perceive the shadow of the Cross looming over their solemn gathering that night. Jesus did; and even though, humanly speaking, he shrank from it, still he yearned for it with all his Heart because this was how we would be saved. During his ministry, Jesus had told his disciples, "For the Son of man also came not to be served but to serve, and to give his life as a ransom for many" (Mk 10:45). And, as his Passion drew near, he said, "For this reason the Father loves me, because I lay down my life, that I may take it again. No one takes it from me, but I lay it down of my own accord. I have power to lay it down, and I have power to take it again; this charge I have received from my Father" (Jn 10:17–18). Christ is the Lamb of God, whose Blood marks the lintel of the world, and by this Blood God liberates us from death.

What Christ did by those words was to change, not the action, but its meaning: "Do this in remembrance of *me*." The blessing and breaking of bread, the blessing and sharing of wine would still be done as before. But now, it was not the Exodus that would become present, it would be Jesus himself and his saving sacrifice. This is why Saint Paul reminded the Corinthians, "For as often as you eat this bread and drink the chalice, you proclaim the Lord's death until he comes" (1 Cor 11:26). To whom do we proclaim the Lord's death? First, to the Father, at whose command Jesus laid down his life. We proclaim it in thanksgiving, blessing the Father for this ultimate expression of his merciful love.

And we proclaim it to one another, because it is faith in Christ that unites us as members of his Body; our union with him invites us to imitate his sacrificial love for one another.

After speaking of the Lord's Supper as the proclamation of Christ's death, Paul addresses a serious challenge to the Corinthians: "Whoever, therefore, eats the bread or drinks the cup of the Lord in an unworthy manner will be guilty of profaning the body and blood of the Lord. Let a man examine himself, and so eat of the bread and drink of the cup. For any one who eats and drinks without discerning the body eats and drinks judgment upon himself" (1 Cor 11:27–29). What does Paul mean by "discerning the body"? He had already told them in the previous chapter: "The cup of blessing which we bless, is it not a participation in the blood of Christ? The bread which we break, is it not a participation in the body of Christ? Because there is one bread, we who are many are one body, for we all partake of the one bread" (1 Cor 10:16–17). They were to discern Christ's Body present under the forms of bread and wine, a presence inextricably linked to his sacrifice; and they were to discern Christ's Body in the community of believers, a presence inextricably linked to mutual charity.

In just a few short verses, written within thirty years of the Last Supper itself, Saint Paul offers a wealth of theological insight into the meaning of the Eucharist and articulates fundamental ideas that will shape the Eucharistic Prayers in general and the Roman Canon in particular. I would identify the following three:

1. The Eucharistic Prayer is an expression of thanksgiving, blessing the Father for his work of salvation and looking

forward to the fulfillment of that work. The prayer of the Jews highlighted the Passover and anticipated the coming of the Christ. For Christians, the paschal mystery of Jesus' death and Resurrection is the climactic act in God's saving work, and we look forward to the Messiah's return in glory.

2. Our thanksgiving is expressed in the highest form of praise, the offering of sacrifice. It is Christ's own sacrifice that we offer; we can do this because the Eucharist is truly his Body and Blood and because we are truly members of his Body. But it is also our sacrifice, because we unite our self-offering to his: "Come to him, to that living stone, rejected by men but in God's sight chosen and precious; and like living stones be yourselves built into a spiritual house, to be a holy priesthood, to offer spiritual sacrifices acceptable to God through Jesus Christ" (1 Pet 2:4–5). As Christ's sacrifice, it is perfect and all-sufficient; as our sacrifice, it is acceptable to the extent that we make it real by mutual charity.

3. So, whenever we approach God, we pray not only for ourselves, but for one another; even as we ask God to bless us, we intercede for others. Our communion with Christ makes us mindful of our communion with all the members of his Body, the Church.

From these three fundamental themes—thanksgiving, offering, intercession—the composers of the Roman Canon have created a symphony of praise. The three themes continually reappear and intermingle; throughout the piece, like an underlying bass note, sounds the phrase "through Christ our Lord". This is Christ's one perfect sacrifice, which incorporates within it all the offerings made under the old covenant and the self-offerings of the martyrs of the new covenant as well. Our attention is drawn first heavenward, then back to earth, and then back to heaven; our horizon is as wide as the universal Church, but we also pause to pray for those who are dear to us and for ourselves as poor sinners.

As we consider the Canon as a whole, we might see it in this way: at the heart of the prayer is enshrined the pearl of great price, the Institution Narrative/Memorial/Offering [89–92].[2] By calling to mind the paschal mystery, Christ's death and Resurrection become present in our midst, our gifts become his Body and Blood, and we unite our offering to his perfect sacrifice. The rest of the Canon surrounds this mystery. We begin with an initial prayer of praise for God's saving work, uniting our praise with that of the angels [83]. Seeing the great love the Father has shown us, we dare to approach him and ask him to accept our offerings [84]. We are offering our sacrifice for the universal Church and for those who are dear to us [84–85]. As we pray for one another, we pray in communion with the saints, asking God to protect us in answer to their prayers [86]. What are we praying for? Primarily, for peace and salvation, now and hereafter [87]. Then, on the verge of the Institution Narrative, we beg God to consecrate our gifts of bread and wine, so that they may become the Body and Blood of Christ [88]. After the consecration, we again ask God to accept our offering. Why? Christ's sacrifice is perfect and has been accepted; but our own offering has value only to the extent we truly offer ourselves, and so we call to mind some great Old Testament figures to learn from their example [93]. The

---

[2] Throughout this book, the numbers in brackets correspond to those given to the various prayers of the Roman Canon in the *Roman Missal.*

reason that our offering is accepted is that it is united with Christ's eternal sacrifice in heaven [94]. Our thought of the world to come encourages us to pray for those who have died, and also for ourselves, asking that we be admitted into the company of the saints [95–96]. As our thoughts turn back to earth, we acknowledge all God's earthly blessings [97]. The Canon ends with a resounding doxology: all of creation, all of history, forever glorifies the Father through, with, and in Christ, in the unity of the Holy Spirit [98].

This is a very brief sketch; in the subsequent chapters, we will meditate on each of the prayers in turn. I would like to conclude this introduction by saying a word about the poetic flavor that pervades the Canon as a whole and, then, something about its theology. As to the poetry, it is clear that those who composed and edited this prayer had the Roman genius for engineering, but they also had an ear for cadence. This rhythm defies translation into English, but some aware-ness of it can help us appreciate the phrases that may strike us as repetitious. The Canon employs a poetic device found commonly in Hebrew poetry, especially the Psalms: paral-lelism. Sometimes the pattern is double: *rogámus ac pétimus; de tuis donis ac datis;* sometimes triple: *haec dona, haec múnera, haec sancta sacrifícia illibáta;* sometimes fourfold: *pacificáre, cus-todíre, adunáre et régere dignéris;* and even fivefold: *benedíctam, adscríptam, ratam, rationábilem, acceptabilémque.* (The meaning of these phrases will be examined as they occur; they are given here to suggest the rhythm of the prayers in Latin.) As in Hebrew poetry, sometimes the subsequent word sim-ply echoes the first, at other times it complements it or of-fers a contrast. These poetic repetitions are not initially to everyone's taste, and it may be that one reason Eucharistic Prayer II is used so often is that it is so concise. But since the Eucharistic Prayer is the heart of the Mass, it is certainly fitting from time to time to give voice to this poetic praise of God.

To whom is this "praise of God" addressed? Not simply to God, but to God the Father. He is called *Dómine, sancte Pater, omnípotens aetérne Deus* (Lord, holy Father, almighty, eternal God) at the beginning of the Preface [83], and he is addressed by those various titles all through the Eucharistic Prayer. The Roman Canon breathes an atmosphere of awe in God's presence, which serves as a check to excessive familiarity. However, surrounded by angelic choirs as he is, and approached with due reverence and respect by us as he deserves, God is above all the *clementíssime Pater*, the most merciful Father, into whose presence we come with confidence through Christ our Lord [84]. Christ is our Mediator with the Father: ten times the phrase "through Christ" or its equivalent appears in the Canon. Only once is Christ referred to explicitly as God ("Mary, Mother of our God and Lord, Jesus Christ" [86]), but the use of the term "Lord" for both God the Father and Christ affirms the Son's full divinity.

What of the Holy Spirit? Apart from the final doxology, the Spirit is never mentioned. For some, this is a glaring deficiency, but I would suggest the reason is not neglect of the Holy Spirit; quite the opposite. The following exercise may help us to appreciate the role of the Holy Spirit in the Roman Canon: Someone says to you, "Go into the next room and count how many people are there." You return and report, "Six." But you could be one person short. Did you include yourself in the count? Similarly, we might be tempted to say that the Canon speaks about two of the three Persons of the Holy Trinity; but we are not adverting to the speaker. The "we" who pray throughout the Canon (and it is always "we", never "I") is not only the priest and congregation gathered in a particular church or even just the communion of all believers throughout the world. It is the Holy Spirit who prays in us; he is not the object of our prayer; he is the one who utters it. The Holy Spirit is the bond of love uniting us with Christ, enabling us to approach the Father through the Son. The Holy Spirit is the bond of love between the Father and the Son, which is why Christ is our one, perfect Mediator. It is by the Holy Spirit that all the blessings that come to us through Christ reach us (and that includes the sanctifying word of Christ that transforms the bread and wine into his Body and Blood). The Holy Spirit is not forgotten—he is acting so intimately in the prayer that there is no need to refer to his presence.

In speaking of the Roman Canon, the Council of Trent taught that it contains only "what savors in the highest degree of that holiness and devotion which raises its offerers' minds to God".[3] The word "savors", *redoleat*, means to "diffuse a fragrance". This image of perfume expresses well the subtle action of the Holy Spirit in the Eucharistic liturgy. Our sense of smell is in some ways the most elusive of our senses but is also the sense with the greatest memory: the hint of a scent can rekindle experiences from our distant past. As we open the door and enter the holy place that is the Roman Canon, let us allow the aroma of the Holy Spirit to summon up for us the images, personalities, and events that flood the mind of the Church when she carries out her Bridegroom's simple imperative: "Do this in memory of me."

[3] *Doctrine on the Most Holy Sacrifice of the Mass*, chap. 4 (author's translation; DS 1745).

I

Enter His Gates with Thanksgiving

(Psalm 100:4)

83. ℣. The Lord be with you. ℟. And with your spirit.
℣. Lift up your hearts. ℟. We lift them up to the Lord.
℣. Let us give thanks to the Lord our God. ℟. It is right
and just.

It is truly right and just, our duty and salvation, always
and everywhere to give you thanks, Lord, holy Father,
almighty, eternal God, through Christ our Lord.

*83. ℣. Dóminus vobíscum. ℟. Et cum spíritu tuo. ℣. Sursum
corda. ℟. Habémus ad Dóminum. ℣. Grátias agámus Dómino
Deo nostro. ℟. Dignum et iustum est.*

*Vere dignum et iustum est, aequum et salutáre, nos tibi sem-
per et ubíque grátias ágere: Dómine, sancte Pater, omnípotens
aetérne Deus: per Christum Dóminum nostrum.*

The solemn dialogue with which the Eucharistic Prayer
opens proclaims that we are standing on the threshold of
the most important part of the Mass. Elsewhere in the liturgy, the priest addresses the community with the simple invitation, "Let us pray." Here, he and the assembly perform
a duet of mutual encouragement to give thanks that finds
its most beautiful expression when the dialogue is sung.
This exchange of words is like the great portal of a Gothic
cathedral, in which the triumphant figure of Christ in glory
welcomes us into his Kingdom: "I am the door; if any one

enters by me, he will be saved, and will go in and out and find pasture" (Jn 10:9). These spare, unadorned phrases bring us back to the Church's infancy; already in the third century, Saint Cyprian commented on the phrase *sursum corda* as a traditional part of the liturgy in his treatise *On the Lord's Prayer.*

℣. *The Lord be with you.* ℟. *And with your spirit.* The opening exchange is familiar, because it appears elsewhere in the liturgy: as a greeting at the beginning of Mass, just before the proclamation of the Gospel, and at the end of the liturgy, before the blessing and dismissal. At these key moments, the liturgy reminds us that our worship is a conspiracy between the priest and the community. We are not simply a group of individuals who happen to be praying in the same place at the same time or an amorphous mob chanting the same slogans. We are a communion of believers who reflect the unity-in-diversity of the Holy Trinity. The references to "Lord" and "Spirit" suggest the words of Saint Paul: "Now there are varieties of gifts, but the same Spirit; and there are varieties of service, but the same Lord; and there are varieties of working, but it is the same God who inspires them all in every one" (1 Cor 12:4–6). The same Spirit vivifies the diverse ministries and charisms in the Church; the same Lord serves the needs of all in a manner tailored for each; the same God inspires our worship and is the goal of our worship. This simple greeting and response reminds us that the entire Eucharistic liturgy is a conversation, an earthly expression of the eternal dialogue of love between the Father, the Son, and the Holy Spirit.

℣. *Lift up your hearts.* ℟. *We lift them up to the Lord.* The priest has asked that the Lord be with us; now he asks us to be with the Lord. *Sursum corda!* In Latin, the two words convey a sense of exhilaration, a tremor of excitement. In a Roman basilica, when the faithful raised their eyes above the altar, they beheld a glittering jeweled cross or a mosaic of Christ and his saints in glory. This simple command compresses into a few words a whole way of life recommended to us by Saint Paul: "If then you have been raised with Christ, seek the things that are above, where Christ is, seated at the right hand of God. Set your minds on things that are above, not on things that are on earth. For you have died, and your life is hidden with Christ in God. When Christ who is our life appears, then you also will appear with him in glory" (Col 3:1–4). As the Roman Canon unfolds, our attention will continually fluctuate between heaven and earth: the Lord is with us here below, and we are with him above —because we are one with the Lord, and wherever he is, there is heaven. Of course, our hearts should always be set on the Lord, but above all as we enter into this, our most solemn prayer.

℣. *Let us give thanks to the Lord our God.* ℟. *It is right and just.* This verse and response has its origin in the Jewish meal blessings. Those blessings recalled God's benefits in creation and redemption; they form the nucleus for our Christian *Eucharistic* Prayers, that is, prayers of *thanksgiving*. We give thanks because we are able to lift up our hearts to the Lord, and we want to come into God's presence especially to thank him for his providential care and the gift of salvation. *It is right and just* translates the words of the Jewish blessing, but its Latin rendering, *dignum et iustum est*, also has echoes of the ancient Roman culture: acclamations like this were a way for the community to endorse an important decision or an election. By these words, the worshipping assembly expresses support for its priest, who is about to proclaim

the great prayer of thanksgiving in its name. Like the acclamation *Amen* at the conclusion of liturgical prayers, this
phrase ratifies what the priest proclaims at the altar. Priest
and people are distinct, but united—another echo of the
communion at the heart of the mystery of the Trinity. The
obligation to offer God thanks that is *dignum* was mentioned
by Saint Paul: "We are bound to give thanks to God always
for you, brethren, *as is fitting*, because your faith is growing
abundantly, and the love of every one of you for one another
is increasing" (2 Thess 1:3).

*It is truly right and just, our duty and salvation, always and
everywhere to give you thanks, Lord, holy Father, almighty, eternal God, through Christ our Lord.* The priest in turn ratifies
the sentiments of the community and expands upon them:
"It certainly *is* right and just to give thanks . . . in fact, not
only is it our duty to God, it is beneficial to us." Gratitude
is *salutáre*, a wholesome virtue, because it shows we realize that we have received something from another, and we
cherish the gift. How different is the attitude of those who
forget this: "What have you that you did not receive? If then
you received it, why do you boast as if it were not a gift?"
(1 Cor 4:7). Gratitude is salvific because it conforms us to
Christ, the Son of God, who knows that all that he is and all
that he has is the Father's gift to him. This sense of gratitude
should mark us *always and everywhere*, as the Apostle exhorts
us: "Rejoice always, pray constantly, give thanks in all circumstances; for this is the will of God in Christ Jesus for
you" (1 Thess 5:16–18). It is easy to give thanks when things
are going well, although we probably do not do it as often
as we should. To give thanks in the face of a family tragedy,
a debilitating illness, or some other calamity requires great
faith, faith that we are still held in God's merciful hands and

that he continues to lavish blessings upon us. It is a great so-
lace for us as Catholics that we can gather around the Lord's
table daily to give thanks, in bad times as well as good. And
we give thanks by celebrating the Eucharist, the meal that
proclaims the death of the Lord. At first sight, it may seem
strange that Paul singled out that particular moment in Jesus'
life to associate with this great prayer of thanks; but by the
power of his Resurrection, Christ shows us that the most
senseless, cruel, and seemingly final of tragedies was in fact
the gateway to blessings beyond our imagining.

Yes, we should give thanks always and everywhere—but
why are we gathered to give thanks here and now? Quite simply, for the gift of eternal life that we have received through
the death and Resurrection of Christ and for the outpour-
ing of the Holy Spirit. The first Christians, inspired by the
Jewish prayers of thanksgiving for the Exodus, celebrated
the "memorial" of Christ by praising God for his saving
work. Echoes of these prayers can be discerned throughout
the Epistles, but the beginning of the Letter to the Ephesians
offers a particularly rich model:

> Blessed be the God and Father of our Lord Jesus Christ,
> who has blessed us in Christ with every spiritual blessing
> in the heavenly places, even as he chose us in him before
> the foundation of the world, that we should be holy and
> blameless before him. He destined us in love to be his sons
> through Jesus Christ, according to the purpose of his will,
> to the praise of his glorious grace which he freely bestowed
> on us in the Beloved. In him we have redemption through
> his blood, the forgiveness of our trespasses, according to
> the riches of his grace which he lavished upon us. For
> he has made known to us in all wisdom and insight the
> mystery of his will, according to his purpose which he set

forth in Christ as a plan for the fulness of time, to unite
all things in him, things in heaven and things on earth.
(Eph 1:3–10)

Most other Eucharistic Prayers narrate the broad sweep
of salvation history; the Roman Canon takes a distinctive
approach. As the priest begins the great prayer of thanksgiving, the motive for our praise is expressed in this first
major component of the Canon, which highlights a particular aspect of the paschal mystery according to the occasion or season of the year. This is the first, and most
significant, of the variable parts of the Roman Canon. It
is an essential part of the Canon, although it might seem
to be merely a prologue to it. The name given to this section, the Preface, contributed to this dissociation. The Latin
word *praefatio* has a complex history: it can mean "to speak
something beforehand" (the origin of our English word
"preface"), or it can mean "to speak something before an
audience" (somewhat akin to our word "proclaim"). In ancient times a *praefatio* could be a formula of solemn prayer,
and sometimes the word was used for the Roman Eucharistic
Prayer as a whole. When the Roman Canon was adopted in
Gaul, the Gallican tradition of creating a Eucharistic Prayer
by connecting together a series of orations influenced their
understanding of the Canon: "Prayer Six" extended from
the *Sanctus* to the Lord's Prayer, so "Prayer Five" came to
be viewed as a preliminary to the Eucharistic Prayer as such.
This cleavage widened as the custom grew of reciting the
prayers after the *Sanctus* quietly (whereas the Preface was
always said or sung aloud), and when the "T" of *Te ígitur*
was expanded into a large initial and eventually became a
full-page illustration of Christ crucified.

Enter His Gates with Thanksgiving

It is important to stress the integral place of the Preface in the Canon, because in the Roman liturgy the expressions of thanksgiving (*eucharistia*) are concentrated in this section of the Eucharistic Prayer. It is also the part of the Canon that provided a space for creativity after the rest of the text became fixed at the end of the sixth century. Over the centuries, there have been conflicting tendencies to expand or restrict the number of Prefaces. The seventh-century Leonine Sacramentary contains 267 Prefaces, and the Ambrosian Rite in Milan has a separate Preface for every celebration. In the ninth century the Roman Rite limited the repertoire to nine Prefaces, which gradually expanded again to twenty-five. Since the Second Vatican Council, the number of Prefaces in the Roman liturgy has grown significantly.

Not only is the Preface a part of the Eucharistic Prayer, it is, properly speaking, the beginning of the Prayer. The priest is no longer addressing the community; rather, he is addressing God, and he will continue to do so until the people's "Amen" concludes the Canon. And, as the solemnity of this Prayer was suggested by its elaborate introductory dialogue, so here God is addressed by a cluster, almost a litany, of titles: *Lord, holy Father, almighty, eternal God.* These names express in microcosm the motives for our gratitude. We give thanks for our very existence by addressing the eternal, all-powerful Creator, who is infinitely greater than all he has made, "the blessed and only Sovereign, the King of kings and Lord of lords, who alone has immortality and dwells in unapproachable light, whom no man has ever seen or can see" (1 Tim 6:16). The Roman Canon repeatedly stresses the majesty and transcendence of God. But this transcendent God freely chose to enter into the history of a people. This was revealed in a dramatic way when, standing before

the burning bush, Moses asked God his name: "God said
to Moses, 'I AM WHO I AM.' And he said, 'Say this to the
people of Israel, "I AM has sent me to you."' God also said
to Moses, 'Say this to the sons of Israel, "The LORD, the
God of your fathers, the God of Abraham, the God of Isaac,
and the God of Jacob, has sent me to you": this is my name
for ever, and thus I am to be remembered throughout all
generations'" (Ex 3:14–15). He who alone IS, *omnípotens,
aetérne Deus*, is also *Dómine*, the LORD, the God of Abraham,
Isaac, and Jacob. We are addressing the same God to whom
Jesus and the disciples gave thanks at the Last Supper for
the blessings of creation and for his saving work in Israel's
history.

However, there is something radically new about our
prayer, and the other title alludes to it: *sancte Pater*. This was
the form of address used by Jesus himself when he prayed
at the end of the Supper: "Holy Father, keep them in your
name, which you have given me, that they may be one, even
as we are one" (Jn 17:11). We come into the presence of
the Creator of the universe and the Lord of history *through
Christ our Lord*. This is a distinctive element of Christian
prayer. Sacred Scripture exhorts us to offer our praise and
thanks to the Father through Christ: "Through him then let
us continually offer up a sacrifice of praise to God . . ." (Heb
13:15); ". . . do everything in the name of the Lord Jesus,
giving thanks to God the Father through him" (Col 3:17).
Christ is our eternal High Priest: "Consequently he is able
for all time to save those who draw near to God through
him, since he always lives to make intercession for them"
(Heb 7:25). He who is the Priest is also the Sacrifice that
gives us access to the Father: "Therefore, brethren, since
we have confidence to enter the sanctuary by the blood of

Jesus, by the new and living way which he opened for us through the curtain, that is, through his flesh, and since we have a great priest over the house of God, let us draw near with a true heart in full assurance of faith" (Heb 10:19–22). The conviction that Christ is our Mediator with the Father is at the heart of Christian faith, and it is a theme that recurs continually in the Roman Canon.

Christ is our Mediator first by virtue of the Incarnation: he is the eternal Son who put aside his divine glory and humbled himself to become our brother. He is truly God by nature and, also, one of us. When Jesus addressed God as *holy Father*, he prayed for his disciples, "that they may be one, even as we are one". Later in the same prayer, he expanded on this idea, "The glory which you have given me I have given to them, that they may be one even as we are one, I in them and you in me, that they may become perfectly one, so that the world may know that you have sent me and have loved them even as you have loved me" (Jn 17:22–23). Our communion with one another and our communion with God are both rooted in Christ: this is what makes the Eucharist a "Holy Communion". The meeting point of these two axes, our horizontal oneness with one another and our vertical oneness with God, forms the Cross. This was why the Father sent Jesus and how he showed us that he loves us even as he loves Christ. When we profess, "God so loved the world that he gave his only-begotten Son" (Jn 3:16), we must recall that he did not just give him to us as a teacher or a guide; he gave him over to death for our sake. By becoming Man, the Son did the one thing he could not do for us as God: he died for us. The communion of the Lord's Supper is indissolubly linked to the Body given for us, the Blood shed for us. "For there is one God, and there is one mediator between God and men, the man Christ Jesus, who gave himself as a ransom for all" (1 Tim 2:5).

Christ is our Mediator with the Father, and we offer our praise and thanks through him; in the next chapter we shall see that the angels do so, too. But he is also the Father's Mediator to us, and many of the Prefaces speak of how the Father showers his love on us *through Christ our Lord*. Here are a few examples:

> Through him the holy exchange that is our ransom from sin today is made clear: as your Word takes unto himself our sinful weakness, not only is our mortal human nature itself promoted to a state of everlasting honor, but because of the marvelous unity it now shares with the divine, that human nature renders us deathless as well. (Christmas Preface 3)

> For by means of the saving suffering of your Son the entire world has come to understand what it means to proclaim your divine majesty, while through the unspeakable force of the Cross it becomes clear what judgment the world deserves, what mighty power the Crucified One wields. (Preface of the Lord's Passion 1)

> Through him the children of the light rise to eternal life, and for his faithful the halls of the heavenly kingdom are opened wide. For the death we are subject to is ransomed by his death; and in his resurrection the life of everyone has arisen. (Easter Preface 2)

> Through your most beloved Son, in great kindliness do you restore the human race, just as you established it in the beginning. Thus it is fitting that all creatures serve you, that all who have been redeemed duly praise you, that your Saints be one at heart in blessing you. (Common Preface 3)

For through him you have brought us to a knowledge of your truth, so that we might be made into his body by the bond of one faith and one baptism. Through him you poured forth your Holy Spirit on all peoples. Through the variety of gifts that he gives, the Spirit does marvelous deeds and brings about unity; dwelling in the children of adoption, the Spirit fills and rules the entire Church. (The Unity of Christians)

The Prefaces in the Roman liturgy celebrate how God's saving plan was fulfilled in the paschal mystery of Christ's Incarnation, life, death, Resurrection, Ascension, and the sending of the Holy Spirit. In a few short lines they provide rich fare for reflection, and we would do well from time to time to meditate on one or another of them. *Through Christ our Lord*: the Roman Canon is a celebration of Christ our High Priest, our one Mediator with the Father. Through him our praise and thanks ascend to God; praise and thanks for all the blessings that have descended upon us and continue to descend upon us through Christ. He is Jacob's Ladder, as he himself said: "Truly, truly, I say to you, you will see heaven opened, and the angels of God ascending and descending upon the Son of Man" (Jn 1:51). And as we lift up our hearts, we find ourselves in the company of those angels.

II

Day and Night They Never
Cease to Sing, "Holy, Holy, Holy"
(Revelation 4:8)

Through him the Angels praise your majesty,
Dominations adore and Powers tremble before you.
Heaven and the Virtues of heaven and the blessed Seraphim
worship together with exultation.
May our voices, we pray, join with theirs
in humble praise, as we acclaim:[1]

Holy, Holy, Holy Lord God of hosts.
Heaven and earth are full of your glory. Hosanna in the
  highest.
Blessed is he who comes in the name of the Lord.
Hosanna in the highest.

Per quem maiestátem tuam laudant Angeli, adórant Domina-
tiónes, tremunt Potestátes. Caeli caelorúmque Virtútes, ac beáta
Séraphim, sócia exsultatióne concélebrant. Cum quibus et nostras
voces ut admítti iúbeas, deprecámur, súpplici confessióne dicéntes:

Sanctus, Sanctus, Sanctus Dóminus Deus Sabaóth.
Pleni sunt caeli et terra glória tua.
Hosánna in excélsis.

---

[1] This concluding paragraph is used in several Prefaces: Lent 4, Common Preface 2, Blessed Virgin Mary 1, Saint Joseph, and the Exaltation
of the Holy Cross. Other Prefaces name the angelic powers in a variety
of ways.

In Memory of Me

Benedíctus qui venit in nómine Dómini.
Hosánna in excélsis.

The Letter to the Hebrews is the principal source for our
theology of Christ the High Priest; it also provides some of
the most vivid descriptions of the heavenly liturgy. Here is
how it paints the scene that meets us as we near the end of
the Preface:

> But you have come to Mount Zion and to the city of the
> living God, the heavenly Jerusalem, and to innumerable
> angels in festal gathering, and to the assembly of the first-
> born who are enrolled in heaven, and to a judge who is
> God of all, and to the spirits of just men made perfect,
> and to Jesus, the mediator of a new covenant, and to the
> sprinkled blood that speaks more graciously than the blood
> of Abel. (Heb 12:22–24)

The angels, too, offer their praise *through him*. Christ's supe-
riority to the angels is treated extensively at the beginning
of the Letter to the Hebrews, and in First Peter we read
that the risen Lord "has gone into heaven and is at the right
hand of God, with angels, authorities, and powers subject
to him" (1 Pet 3:22).

Angels appear throughout the entire Bible, from the cherubim guarding the way to the tree of life at the beginning
of Genesis (3:24) to the angel at the end of the Book of
Revelation who showed the Seer his visions (22:8). While
individual angels are entrusted with missions in the execution of God's saving plan, whenever they are described as
praising God, it is always in vast throngs:

A stream of fire issued
  and came forth from before him;

a thousand thousands served him,
and ten thousand times ten thousand stood before him.
(Dan 7:10)

We should not imagine that these multitudes are a mob of spiritual "extras" conjured up to create impressive crowd scenes: each one of these "innumerable angels" praises a different perfection of God, some unique facet of his divine glory. We know very little about the angelic nature; but when we compare ourselves as human beings with other earthly creatures, we see that our soul imparts to us an utterly unique personal identity. Angels are pure spirits, and as such they are even more exceptionally personal creatures than we are. We might compare our being taken up into the angelic worship, if it is not irreverent, to the experience of a cat or dog in church during Mass. Such animals are sensitive to their surroundings and, to some degree, to human actions and moods—which is why we keep them as pets— but there is a great chasm between our natures and theirs. Similarly, the glory of the angels eludes us, because their natures are so far superior to ours. One thing we do share with them is this: the desire to praise our Maker.

As we are borne up to the heavenly Jerusalem on wings of praise and thanksgiving, the concluding words of the different Prefaces describe the various spiritual beings mentioned in Scripture wheeling in and out of joyous formations: Angels (1 Pet 3:22), Archangels (1 Thess 4:16), Dominations, Powers, and Virtues (Eph 1:21), Heavens (Dan 3:36), Thrones (Col 1:16), Cherubim (Ps 99:1), and Seraphim (Is 6:2). Although the Roman Canon is usually marked by a mood of sobriety, there are moments when its authors betray a sense of being overwhelmed by the splendor of the heavenly vision. The attempt to convey something of angelic worship is an example: the choirs of angels are not carefully delineated by rank—the different Prefaces mention them in diverse combinations, like brief impressions scribbled on a postcard written from an exotic land.

Captivated by the beauty of angelic praise, we humbly ask to blend our voices with theirs as ceaselessly they sing . . . and then, in fact, we too sing: "*Holy, holy, holy Lord God of hosts. Heaven and earth are full of your glory.*" The triple *Sanctus* is found in almost all the Eucharistic liturgies of East and West and was mentioned as far back as the end of the first century in the Epistle of Clement of Rome (chap. 34). The first part of this acclamation appears in Isaiah's vision of God in the Temple:

> In the year that King Uzziah died I saw the Lord sitting upon a throne, high and lifted up; and his train filled the temple. Above him stood the seraphim; each had six wings: with two he covered his face, and with two he covered his feet, and with two he flew. And one called to another and said:
>
>> "Holy, holy, holy is the LORD of hosts;
>> the whole earth is full of his glory." (Is 6:1–3)

The Christian liturgies add the word "heaven" to earth: no longer is it just the Temple that resounds with God's praises, nor is it only the seraphim who cry out to one another. Heaven itself is the locus of worship, and all the choirs of heavenly spirits join in. More than that: the word *sabaoth*, kept in Hebrew in the Latin text and translated as "hosts" in English, is a mysterious word with several meanings in the Bible. It can refer to celestial bodies, such as the moon, the sun, and the stars: "Thus the heavens and the earth were finished, and all the host of them" (Gen 2:1); or human armies: "I will lay my hand upon Egypt and bring forth my hosts, my people the sons of Israel, out of the land of Egypt" (Ex 7:4); or angelic forces: "I saw the LORD sitting on his throne, and all the host of heaven standing beside him" (1 Kings 22:19). All creation, visible and invisible, material, human, and angelic, unites in acclaiming the ineffable sanctity of God. Here below, all of us gathered for worship echo with mingled awe and joy that cosmic praise of the triune God: "Holy! Holy! Holy!"

Another melody intermingles with the angelic praises. Children's voices, rising up from the dusty streets of a city in Judea, proclaim: "*Hosanna in the highest. Blessed is he who comes in the name of the Lord. Hosanna in the highest.*" Isaiah feared he would die as he beheld a glimpse of heaven's glory; the liturgy associates that splendor with the image of a poor man riding a donkey. The disparity between celestial splendor and the worn garments and withering branches of Palm Sunday is striking, but we must bear several things in mind. First, it is not without precedent: if in the final days of Christ's earthly life the streets resounded with "*Hosánna in excélsis!*" we recall that the first time a multitude of the heavenly host praise God in the New Testament is with the acclamation "*Glória in excélsis!*" when the newborn Son of God was wrapped in swaddling cloths and laid in a trough for feeding animals. Second, the crowds did the best they could to honor Jesus; their worship should be judged, not by its external magnificence, but by its heartfelt devotion. Finally, in a sense the disparity is God's own doing—the eternal Son of God freely embraced the limitations of our human nature and chose to be born in a stable rather than a palace. Certainly we should give of our best in all that pertains to the worship of God; certainly, even our best falls far short of what he deserves; but just as certainly, our sincere and wholehearted praise is as welcome by him as even the most splendid of angelic songs.

Let us pause for a moment to reflect on this Palm Sunday acclamation. The crowds that welcomed Jesus were quoting a line from Psalm 118:

> Save us, we beg you, O LORD!
> O LORD, we beg you, give us success!
> Blessed be he who enters in the name of the LORD!
> (Ps 118:25–26)

The phrase "Save us, we beg you," is a translation of the Hebrew *Hoshana*; in the next verse, the psalm speaks of going in festal procession with branches, so its use on the occasion was very apt. In fact, the entire psalm is applicable to the life of Jesus and is one of the psalms most often quoted in the New Testament. It is a song of triumph, telling the story of a man, pressed in on every side by his enemies and almost done in, who was rescued by God. The people's destiny was somehow linked to his, and the throng rejoiced in his deliverance as they processed up to the Temple. Psalm 118 is last of the six *Hallel* psalms, which were prayed on festive occasions, and it is very likely that this is what Jesus and the disciples sang at the end of the Last Supper (Mt 26:30; Mk 14:26). The Apostles were probably thinking that evening of the words shouted by the people on the previous Sunday; other verses in the psalm must have filled Jesus with dread as he made his way to Gethsemane: "All nations surrounded me. . . . They surrounded me, surrounded me on every side. . . . They surrounded me like bees, they blazed like a fire of thorns" (Ps 118:10–12). But the psalm goes on to celebrate God's wondrous intervention: the Lord's right hand has struck with power and brought salvation. Psalm 118 became for the first Christians the great Easter Psalm, and three verses in particular appear often in the New Testament and in the Easter liturgies of East and West:

The stone which the builders rejected
   has become the cornerstone.
This is the LORD's doing;
   it is marvelous in our eyes.
This is the day which the LORD has made;
   let us rejoice and be glad in it. (Ps 118:22–24)

Blessed is he who comes in the name of the Lord. Whenever we gather to celebrate the Eucharist, we do so in expectation of the Second Coming of Christ: "For as often as you eat this bread and drink the chalice, you proclaim the Lord's death *until he comes*" (1 Cor 11:26). Paul ends this Epistle with a plea: "Our Lord, come!" (1 Cor 16:23). The last book of the Bible ends with a similar entreaty (Rev 22:20). Paul uses an Aramaic word, *maranatha*, a word also found at the end of the *Didache*, a work that may preserve a Eucharistic text from the end of the New Testament era. It is clear that for the first Christians, their celebration of the Eucharist did not only look back to the Last Supper and Calvary; it also looked ahead to the Lord's return. When he does return, the glory of the angelic praise that surrounds him will be manifest to all, as he himself said: "When the Son of man comes in his glory, and all the angels with him, then he will sit on his glorious throne" (Mt 25:31).

Meanwhile, Christ comes to us here and now in the Eucharist, and we sing the *Sanctus* to welcome him. He comes in the liturgy the way he came that first Christmas—in obscurity, poverty, and simplicity. The sign given to the shepherds was very ordinary: a newborn baby wrapped in swaddling cloths and lying in a manger. The sign given to us, too, is ordinary: plain bread and a cup of wine. But the reality underlying both signs is the same, the Son of God made man. As we contemplate him in our midst, let us listen attentively to hear what only the shepherds heard that Christmas night, the heavenly host praising God.

III

Upon His Long Robe the
Whole World Was Depicted
(Wisdom 18:24)

84. To you, therefore, most merciful Father, we make
humble prayer and petition through Jesus Christ, your
Son, our Lord: that you accept and bless these gifts, these
offerings, these holy and unblemished sacrifices, which we
offer you firstly for your holy Catholic Church. Be pleased
to grant her peace, to guard, unite and govern her throughout the whole world, together with your servant N. our
Pope and N. our Bishop, and all those who, holding to
the truth, hand on the catholic and apostolic faith.

84. Te ígitur, clementíssime Pater, per Iesum Christum, Fílium
tuum, Dóminum nostrum, súpplices rogámus ac pétimus, uti
accépta hábeas et benedícas haec dona, haec múnera, haec sancta
sacrifícia illibáta, in primis, quae tibi offérimus pro Ecclésia tua
sancta cathólica: quam pacificáre, custodíre, adunáre et régere
dignéris toto orbe terrárum: una cum fámulo tuo Papa nostro N.
et Antístite nostro N. et ómnibus orthodóxis atque cathólicae et
apostólicae fídei cultóribus.

The dying echoes of the Palm Sunday acclamation bring us
back to earth, and *therefore* we express our gratitude for the
blessings proclaimed in the Preface by making our offering.
The Mass is a thanksgiving that culminates in the offering of
a gift. The offering itself is so spiritual that it appears to be

only a thanksgiving, but this thanksgiving is the sacrifice of Christ's self-offering. We recall that we are making this offering to our *most merciful Father* through Christ, who is his Son and our Lord: "Blessed be the God and Father of our Lord Jesus Christ, the Father of mercies and God of all comfort" (2 Cor 1:3). As Son, Christ shares the Father's transcendent majesty, whose glory the angels ceaselessly praise; but he is also our brother, one who is like us in all things but sin. So, our boldness in coming into God's presence is prompted by two convictions: the Father is "rich in mercy" (Eph 2:4), and we have a high priest who can sympathize with our weakness. "Let us then with confidence draw near to the throne of grace, that we may receive mercy and find grace to help in time of need" (Heb 4:16). In the Roman Canon, confidence is never reduced to informality; the words *súpplices rogámus ac pétimus* express a spirit of reverent reserve. "We who are suppliants ask, indeed we beg. . . ." Such language appears frequently in the Canon, and its deferential tone may rankle in our egalitarian age. For that very reason this Eucharistic Prayer counters the temptation to be overly familiar in our approach to God. Somewhere C. S. Lewis suggests that many people today do not want a heavenly Father who will care for them, but a heavenly Grandfather who will spoil them. The Letter to the Hebrews urges us to approach the throne of grace with confidence; but it also contains this exhortation: "Let us offer to God acceptable worship, with reverence and awe; for our God is a consuming fire" (Heb 12:28–29).

For what do we ask? *That you accept and bless these gifts.* This seems straightforward enough, but let us consider carefully what we are asking. The request that the Father accept our gifts recurs several times in the Roman Canon. To the extent that what we offer is Christ's sacrifice, there can be no doubt that the Father will accept it—he already has. But to the extent that we are offering our sacrifice with his, or, better, the sacrifice of ourselves in union with his self-offering, then our dispositions matter. The value of the offering cannot substitute for the right interior attitude of the offerers—this is a point made frequently by the prophets and one explicitly ratified by our Lord himself: "Go and learn what this means, 'I desire mercy, and not sacrifice'" (Mt 9:13). In the Sermon on the Mount, he instructs us: "So if you are offering your gift at the altar, and there remember that your brother has something against you, leave your gift there before the altar and go; first be reconciled to your brother, and then come and offer your gift" (Mt 5:23–24). And we should recall that what prompted Saint Paul to bring up the subject of the Eucharist in his Epistle was the scandalous lack of charity among the Corinthians: "When you meet together, it is not the Lord's supper that you eat. For in eating, each one goes ahead with his own meal, and one is hungry and another is drunk" (1 Cor 11:20–21). Our prayer for the acceptance of our gifts is a prayer for conversion of heart, so that, as the ancient instruction given at priestly ordination says, we may imitate the mystery we celebrate. As to our appeal that God bless our offering, this is a request that what happened when Jesus blessed the bread and wine at the Last Supper will happen again—that they will become his Body and Blood. This request becomes more explicit in another prayer [88], and we will reflect on this point later.

We ask God to accept and bless *these gifts, these offerings, these holy and unblemished sacrifices*. Historians of liturgy have offered various interpretations for these three terms. In the Egyptian Liturgy of Saint Mark (which enjoys some kinship with the Roman Canon), there is a parallel prayer that refers to offerings for the dead, offerings for the living, and sacrifices offered to God. Or the three words may be different designations for the same thing: they are gifts (*dona*) being offered in a liturgical act (*múnera*) to God (*sacrificia*). The words *holy and unblemished* are descriptive terms used of offerings throughout Scripture, but in the context of the Mass they clearly allude to Christ's own sacrifice. As far back as the second century, the Fathers have seen the Eucharist as the fulfillment of the prophecy of Malachi 1:11 that in every time and place a pure offering would be made to God. Christ's sacrifice is uniquely holy and unblemished: "You know that you were ransomed from the futile ways inherited from your fathers, not with perishable things such as silver or gold, but with the precious blood of Christ, like that of a lamb without blemish or spot. . . . Through him you have confidence in God, who raised him from the dead and gave him glory, so that your faith and hope are in God" (1 Pet 1:18–21). Again, our confidence comes from approaching the Father through Christ and always associating our offering with his.

The third of our major Eucharistic themes (thanksgiving, offering, intercession) now makes its appearance: *which we offer you firstly for your holy catholic Church*. The preposition *for* links the ideas of offering and petition. It can mean "on behalf of", that is, we recognize that what we do at this altar is not our own private affair; it is united to the one sacrifice offered up from the rising of the sun to its setting by the whole Body of Christ, the Church. It can also mean "for the benefit of", that is, that we are asking God to pour out his blessings on the whole Body of Christ. Two qualities of the Church are mentioned: *holy* and *catholic*. These attributes are not a condition generated by her members; they are God's gift. Saint Paul teaches that the Church is made holy by her union with Christ: "Christ loved the Church and gave himself up for her, that he might sanctify her, having cleansed her by the washing of water with the word, that he might present the Church to himself in splendor, without spot or wrinkle or any such thing, that she might be holy and without blemish" (Eph 5:25–27). The Church becomes unblemished through Christ's unblemished sacrifice. But holiness is not a static condition. The Church grows in holiness the more we who gather around the altar imitate Christ's self-sacrificing love. And we can understand *catholic* to be more than a geographical term: every part of creation, every element of human society, and every corner of our individual lives should pulsate with the love of God.

We realize that certain conditions are needed for the Church's holiness and universality to come to maturity, so we ask God: *Be pleased to grant her peace, to guard, unite and govern her throughout the whole world.* This is the very prayer of Jesus himself at the Last Supper. On that occasion he told his disciples, "Peace I leave with you; my peace I give to you; not as the world gives do I give to you" (Jn 14:27). He made it very clear—and this at the meal where he linked the breaking of the bread and the sharing of the cup with his own approaching death—that this peace would not mean an absence of conflict. On the contrary, he warned them that they would be hated because of him. What, then, will be the source of their peace? Communion: his communion with the Father, their communion individually with him, and their communion with one another in him. He concluded the discourse with words that are both frank and encouraging: "The hour is coming, indeed it has come, when you will be scattered, every man to his home, and will leave me alone; yet I am not alone, for the Father is with me. I have said this to you, that in me you may have peace. In the world you have tribulation; but be of good cheer, I have overcome the world" (Jn 16:32–33). And then he prayed for precisely what we now ask: that the Father would safeguard and unite his followers: "Holy Father, keep them in your name, which you have given me, that they may be one, even as we are one. While I was with them, I kept them in your name, which you have given me; I have guarded them. . . . I do not pray that you should take them out of the world, but that you should keep them from the evil one" (Jn 17:11–12, 15).

Our peace derives from being protected, guided, and brought together in unity by the Father because of our union with his Son. This raises a point that may be disturbing, even perhaps scandalous. What unifies believers *throughout the whole world* is what divides us from everyone else: our faith in Christ. In his infancy, it was predicted that Jesus was a sign that would be opposed; in his ministry, he proclaimed that he had come to bring, not peace, but a sword, dividing even those who were closest by natural kinship; and in his prayer at the end of the Last Supper, he said quite plainly: "I am not praying for the world but for those whom you have given me, for they are yours" (Jn 17:9). Christ prays for those who belong to the Father because they are one with him, and this relationship is continually alluded to in the Roman Canon: we pray for *your* Church [84], *your* servants [85], *your* family [87], *your* holy people [92], *your* servants who have died [95]. On the other hand, Christ's prayer does have a limitless horizon: "I do not pray for these only, but also for those who believe in me through their word"

(Jn 17:20). There is an inherent tension: our relationship in Christ makes us one but separates us from others; yet that relationship is also meant to sanctify all creation.

In effect, the seemingly straightforward description *holy catholic Church* contains within it a challenging paradox. In the Old Testament, the people, the Temple, and the priesthood were sanctified by being set apart from the world and dedicated to God. The chosen people avoided contact with Gentiles precisely to safeguard their unique relationship with God. After Christ's Resurrection, this relationship was extended to the nations. As Saint Peter wrote to Gentiles: "But you are a chosen race, a royal priesthood, a holy nation, God's own people, that you may declare the wonderful deeds of him who called you out of darkness into his marvelous light. Once you were no people but now you are God's people; once you had not received mercy but now you have received mercy" (1 Pet 2:9–10). A sect can maintain its purity by insulating itself from the corrosive influence of the world; but if the community of believers is to preach the Gospel to all nations, the sectarian solution is not an option. Again, let us listen to the words of Jesus' prayer at the Last Supper: "I do not pray that you should take them out of the world, but that you should keep them from the evil one. They are not of the world, even as I am not of the world. Sanctify them in the truth; your word is truth. As you sent me into the world, so I have sent them into the world. And for their sake I consecrate myself, that they also may be consecrated in truth" (Jn 17:15–19). It is clear that Jesus wants us to be in the world but not of it; and what sets us apart as holy (this is what the words "sanctify" and "consecrate" mean) is the word of truth that makes us, by the indwelling of the Holy Spirit, his brothers and sisters and, so, the sons and daughters of his Father. The challenge is to be both *holy* and *catholic*, never to lose sight of the fact that the essential foundation for our unity is faith in Christ, but that the awareness of this can never be an excuse simply to take care of our own. The description of Aaron the high priest in the Book of Wisdom is an image of Christ the true Priest and of ourselves who unite our prayer of intercession with his in the Eucharist: "For upon his long robe the whole world was depicted" (Wis 18:24).

This is a perennial dilemma for the Church, which can be tempted either to hold herself aloof from the world or to find herself becoming "worldly". And it is a basic challenge for every believer: When do we embrace the values honored by our culture, and when must we resist them in order to remain true to Christ? Since we are considering this very practical and crucial question while meditating on one of the prayers from the Church's "sacrifice of praise", it is worth noting that Paul himself articulates the challenge we face in liturgical terms: "I appeal to you therefore, brethren, by the mercies of God, to present your bodies as a living sacrifice, holy and acceptable to God, which is your spiritual worship. Do not be conformed to this world but be transformed by the renewal of your mind, that you may prove what is the will of God, what is good and acceptable and perfect" (Rom 12:1–2).

"Communion" can be a nebulous ideal, but the Incarnation imparts to it a concrete reality. The Son of God came into the world at a specific date and in a particular place. The unity for which he prayed at the Last Supper was not some vague sense of goodwill among those who admired his teachings; he was praying for the actual people gathered with him at table and those who would believe in him on the basis of their testimony. They were no heroes, and in fact that very night they abandoned the Lord and scattered, but Christ's prayer was heard: after his Resurrection they came together again and then went out to preach the Gospel. These Apostles founded communities that in turn handed on the Gospel. As we pray for the Church *throughout the whole world*, the Roman Canon gives human features to our petition: *together with your servant N. our Pope and N. our Bishop, and all those who, holding to the truth, hand on the catholic and apostolic faith*. These are the leaders through whom the Holy Spirit directs the Church and holds her together as a visible community. They are the successors of the Twelve who were at table with Jesus on that night two thousand years ago, and his prayer for unity continues to bear fruit in their communion with one another.

The intimate connection between the Eucharist and the bishop in fostering the oneness of the community is very ancient. Writing at the end of the New Testament era, Saint Ignatius of Antioch gave this counsel: "Therefore be careful to take part only in the one Eucharist: there is one flesh of our Lord Jesus Christ, and one cup unto union with his blood; there is one altar and one bishop, together with the presbyters and deacons" (*To the Philadelphians*, 4; author's translation). All of the smaller communities within a local Church (parishes, schools, religious communities, and so on) find a focus of unity in the successor of the Apostles in their midst; this is why the bishop is mentioned by name in every Eucharistic celebration. The bishop also serves as a hinge connecting the local church to the worldwide Catholic communion because he is a member of the college of bishops led by Peter's successor, the Bishop of Rome. Just as the bishop is a visible sign of unity for his local Church, so the pope is a sign of unity for the worldwide Church. This, too, is an ancient teaching, for, writing to the Church at Rome, Ignatius describes her as "worthy of God, worthy of honor, worthy of the highest happiness, worthy of praise, worthy of obtaining her every desire, worthy of being deemed holy, and which presides over love" (*To the Romans*, 1, 1, author's translation). The Roman Church "presides over love" by fostering communion between all the local Churches, and the mention of her shepherd's name in the Canon underscores the fact that the many diverse local Churches truly form one Church. As important as these positions of leadership are, however, the Canon also provides a salutary lesson in humility with that simple letter "N", an abbreviation for "Name". Bishops and popes come and go; the continuity comes from the communities of faith over which they preside for a time.

What unites the various local Churches is not primarily an ecclesiastical structure, but what Christ prayed for at the Last Supper: "Sanctify them in the truth; your word is truth" (Jn 17:17). Hence the description of the shepherds of the Church as *all those who, holding to the truth, hand on the catholic and apostolic faith.* The community of believers is diverse in many ways; what must unite them is a shared faith in Christ and a common understanding of the essentials regarding that faith. Here again, what is a source of communion is also a source of division. Those bishops (and their Churches) are called *orthodoxis* that *hand on the catholic and apostolic faith.* We are praying for those who profess the same Catholic faith and so belong to "the Roman communion". Where does that leave other Christian churches and communities? In one sense, they are not included in this prayer, and we must have the honesty to recognize this. Unity in faith demands an affirmation of the same essential truths; this is a traditional teaching and one that other communions also hold, explicitly or implicitly.

However, the ecumenical advances of the past century invite us to view this question from a different perspective. Formerly, we would say (and other churches would say as well): "We profess the orthodox catholic, apostolic faith; if you do not profess what we do, you are wrong." In a sense, it was all or nothing. But if we start (as the Catholic Church does today) with the idea that there is a real, but imperfect, communion among all Christians, then perhaps this prayer can be understood more inclusively. In his Encyclical *Ut unum sint*, Pope John Paul II reminds us of the teaching of the Second Vatican Council: "Through the celebration of the Eucharist of the Lord in each of these [ancient Eastern] Churches, the Church of God is built up and grows in stature."[1] Churches and Ecclesial Communities of the West ". . . confess Jesus Christ as God and Lord and as the sole Mediator between God and man unto the glory of the one God, Father, Son and Holy Spirit."[2] Elements of the catholic and apostolic faith are handed on in non-Catholic Churches and Communities to a greater or lesser extent. To recognize this is not an invitation to indifferentism or an excuse for avoiding the hard questions of what the essential truths of the faith are, and how they should be determined. But to the extent that we can build on what we share in common with other believers, the unity for which Christ prayed at the Last Supper becomes more a reality. This is not just something to be sought for the sake of good feeling among Christians—it pertains to the very mission of Christ

[1] *Ut unum sint* no. 50, citing *Unitatis Redintegratio* no. 15.
[2] *Ut unum sint* no. 66, citing *Unitatis Redintegratio* no. 20.

himself. This is why he prayed: ". . . that they may all be one; even as you, Father, are in me, and I in you, that they also may be in us, so that the world may believe that you have sent me." (Jn 17:21)

IV

We Have Not Ceased to Pray for You

(Colossians 1:9)

85. Remember, Lord, your servants N. and N. and all gathered here, whose faith and devotion are known to you. For them, we offer you this sacrifice of praise or they offer it for themselves and all who are dear to them, for the redemption of their souls, in hope of health and well-being, and paying their homage to you, the eternal God, living and true.

85. Meménto, Dómine, famulórum famularúmque tuárum N. et N. et ómnium circumstántium, quorum tibi fides cógnita est et nota devótio, pro quibus tibi offérimus: vel qui tibi ófferunt hoc sacrifícium laudis, pro se suísque ómnibus: pro redemptióne animárum suárum, pro spe salútis et incolumitátis suae: tibíque reddunt vota sua aetérno Deo, vivo et vero.

This prayer shifts our attention from the worldwide Church of Christ to our gathering here and now, to those who are offering the sacrifice and to *all who are dear to them*. The ties of friendship and family are precious, and we pause in silent prayer to remember our loved ones who are living (there will be a similar opportunity to pray for our deceased relatives and friends later). They are God's faithful and devoted servants (the Latin specifies both men and women, *famulórum famularúmque*). To be called a faithful servant is high praise:

this was a title given to Abraham, Isaac, and Jacob (2 Mac 1:2), and to Moses (Heb 3:5).

This is a prayer made by those *who offer you this sacrifice of praise*, that is, for the community of believers gathered around this altar here and now. There is a somewhat awkward duplication in the text. The phrase *pro quibus tibi offérimus* ("for whom we offer to you") was added in the ninth century, to be used when a priest was offering Mass for the intentions of persons who were not present. As the prayer stands now, it reminds us that while the priest and people have distinctive roles in the liturgy, we all offer the Eucharistic sacrifice. There are no spectators: everyone is (or should be) actively engaged.

What is it we are doing? *"We offer you this sacrifice of praise . . . and pay . . . homage to you, the eternal God, living and true."* This is almost a verbatim citation from one of the psalms:

"Offer to God a sacrifice of thanksgiving,
    and pay your vows to the Most High;
and call upon me in the day of trouble;
    I will deliver you, and you shall glorify me." (Ps 50:14)

The theme of this psalm is instructive for our worship. God summons his people before him in the presence of his heavenly court to take them to task for their hypocrisy: they punctiliously offer him the prescribed sacrifices, but their conduct is duplicitous and selfish. The Roman Canon replaces the term "the Most High" with the words *the eternal God, living and true*. This title comes from the First Letter to the Thessalonians and helps to bring the lesson home: "They themselves report . . . how you turned to God from idols, to serve a living and true God" (1 Thess 1:9). What in the end is our selfishness but idolatry? We may go through the motions of liturgical worship, all the while worshipping the dead god of our own desires. Once more, our prayer is that our hearts may be converted, that our worship of God will be ratified by our charity.

Psalm 50 ends with God making this promise:

> He who brings thanksgiving as his sacrifice honors me;
>   to him who orders his way aright
>   I will show the salvation of God! (Ps 50:23)

God promises salvation to those who honor him by a thanksgiving sacrifice and order their ways aright. So we offer our sacrifice of praise *for the redemption of [our] souls, in hope of health and well-being.* We pray *for the redemption of [our] souls* because only God can give this:

> Truly no man can ransom himself,
>   or give to God the price of his life,
>   for the ransom of his life [Vulgate: *redemptionis animæ suæ*]
>   is costly. (Ps 49:7–8)

And it is precisely through Christ's self-offering on the Cross that we are redeemed, the same sacrifice that becomes present sacramentally in the Eucharistic liturgy: "You know that you were ransomed from the futile ways inherited from your fathers, not with perishable things such as silver or gold, but with the precious blood of Christ, like that of a lamb without blemish or spot" (1 Pet 1:18–19). Salvation does not concern only the soul; the body, too, shares in it. For this reason we add: *in hope of health and well-being. Spe salútis* can in fact mean either hope of salvation or hope of health, so in the Latin the well-being of the whole person, here and hereafter, is implied. The word *incolumitátis* is similar in Latin to *salútis*, but carries a connotation of "safety". In these two words we pray that the gift of redemption may bring to us and to those who are dear to us eternal salvation, bodily health, and security.

The Roman Canon has an endearing human quality about it. In the midst of majestic prayers that carry us heavenward and speak of the great events of salvation, we pause to pray humbly for ourselves and for those who are dear to us. Our universal vision does not blind us to the needs of those who are particularly confided to our care. The great themes of intercession rightly cry out for our attention—the spread of Christ's Gospel, world peace, the righting of injustices—but God does not despise the intentions that seem insignificant in the global view yet loom large in our own hearts. Jesus taught us to pray for our daily bread and performed his first miracle to save a newly married couple from embarrassment in a little village. The momentary pause in the Canon is filled with these personal intentions. But then, in the prayer that follows, our thoughts are carried beyond even the widest horizons of this world into the foremost ranks of those who have already entered into God's glory.

V

The Smoke of the Incense Rose
with the Prayers of the Saints

(Revelation 8:4)

86. In communion with those whose memory we venerate, especially the glorious ever-Virgin Mary, Mother of our God and Lord, Jesus Christ, and blessed Joseph, her Spouse, your blessed Apostles and Martyrs, Peter and Paul, Andrew, (James, John, Thomas, James, Philip, Bartholomew, Matthew, Simon and Jude: Linus, Cletus, Clement, Sixtus, Cornelius, Cyprian, Lawrence, Chrysogonus, John and Paul, Cosmas and Damian) and all your Saints: we ask that through their merits and prayers, in all things we may be defended by your protecting help. (Through Christ our Lord. Amen.)

86. Communicántes, et memóriam venerántes, in primis gloriósae semper Vírginis Maríae, Genetrícis Dei et Dómini nostri Iesu Christi: sed et beáti Ioseph, eiúsdem Vírginis Sponsi, et beatórum Apostolórum ac Mártyrum tuórum, Petri et Pauli, Andréae, (Iacóbi, Ioánnis, Thomae, Iacóbi, Philíppi, Bartholomaei, Matthaei, Simónis et Thaddaei: Lini, Cleti, Cleméntis, Xysti, Cornélii, Cypriáni, Lauréntii, Chrysógoni, Ioánnis et Pauli, Cosmae et Damiáni) et ómnium Sanctórum tuórum; quorum méritis precibúsque concédas, ut in ómnibus protectiónis tuae muniámur auxílio. (Per Christum Dóminum nostrum. Amen.)

In the fifth chapter of the Book of Revelation, the Lamb who has been slain takes up the sealed scroll and stands before the throne of God. Then we are given a glimpse of the heavenly liturgy:

> And when he had taken the scroll, the four living creatures and the twenty-four elders fell down before the Lamb, each holding a harp, and with golden bowls full of incense, which are the prayers of the saints; and they sang a new song, saying,
>
>> "Worthy are you to take the scroll and to open its seals,
>> for you were slain and by your blood you ransomed men for God
>> from every tribe and tongue and people and nation,
>> and have made them a kingdom and priests to our God,
>> and they shall reign on earth." (Rev 5:8–10)

As we celebrate here below the redemption we receive through the Blood of the Lamb, our prayers mingle with those of the saints, and the worship of the twenty-four elders finds an earthly reflection in the procession of twenty-four Apostles and martyrs led to God's altar by Mary, the Mother of Jesus. We are in communion with the saints just as surely as we are in communion with believers throughout the world, and we approach them with awe and respect, venerating their memory. But just as our worship of God must be seconded by our charity, so our devotion to the saints must be ratified by following their example. With the exception of Mary and Joseph, whose relationship to Jesus was unique, all the saints the Roman Canon sets before us are martyrs—men, women, and children who said Yes to Christ's question: "Are you able to drink the chalice that I drink?" (Mk 10:39). As the twenty-four elders in heaven fall down in worship before the Lamb who was slain, these twenty-four martyrs surround our altar when we offer the Eucharistic sacrifice.

The authors of the Canon present them systematically—twelve Apostles, followed by twelve martyrs. The martyrs are arranged in hierarchical order: six bishops (five of them Roman), then two clerics, and finally four laymen.

They are led by *the glorious ever-Virgin Mary, Mother of our God and Lord, Jesus Christ.* Although she was not literally a martyr, Mary stood beneath the Cross of her Son and united herself completely with his self-offering, so it is fitting that she be accorded special mention in the liturgy where the mystery of the Cross becomes present. (It is noteworthy, too, that the word *especially* translates the Latin *in primis*: this term is used one other time in the Canon, when we ask God to accept the gifts "which we offer you *firstly for* your holy catholic Church" [84]. Mary has a privileged place among the saints and is an image and type of the Church as a whole.) The prayer describes her as the *Mother of our God*, in accord with the dogmatic teaching of the Council of Ephesus (431) that Mary is rightly called *Theotokos*, or Mother of God, because she gave birth to Christ, who is in truth the eternal Son of God. She is not only his Mother, but his preeminent disciple: her total dedication to Christ is signified by another ancient dogma about her enshrined in this prayer, *ever-Virgin*. She has ever been for Christians both a model of faith and a source of comfort when the shadow of the Cross falls across our lives. The last time she is mentioned in the Bible, it is together with Apostles who are named with her in the Canon: "They went up to the upper room, where they were staying, Peter and John and James and Andrew, Philip and Thomas, Bartholomew and Matthew, James the son of Alphaeus and Simon the Zealot and Judas the son

69

of James. All these with one accord devoted themselves to prayer, together with the women and Mary the mother of Jesus, and with his brethren" (Acts 1:13–14). The early Christians were conscious of her presence in their midst; her image appears in the catacombs where the Roman martyrs prayed.

In 1962, Pope John XXIII announced the first significant change in the Roman Canon for many centuries: the addition of the words *and blessed Joseph, her Spouse* to this prayer. This was not a spontaneous gesture (large numbers of the faithful had been petitioning Rome for this addition since the early nineteenth century), but it took many people by surprise. The Canon expresses the devotion of Roman Christians in early times, and veneration of Saint Joseph blossomed only in more recent centuries. Precisely the two dogmas just mentioned in connection with our Lady help to explain the reserve surrounding him in the first centuries: that her child is truly the Son of God and had no human father and that although she and Joseph were married, Mary remained a virgin. Once those truths had taken firm root in the minds of the faithful, devotion to the man closest to Jesus could grow without causing theological confusion. Like Mary, Joseph is a model of a life centered completely on Christ, in circumstances that outwardly appeared very ordinary. To gauge something of the tremendous privilege that was his, we need only consider that Jesus spoke of God as his *abba*: "father" is not an abstract term, and it was the face of the "just man" of Nazareth that Christ associated with that word.

Then come the Apostles, beginning with the twin heroes of Rome, Peter and Paul. Romulus and Remus were the legendary founders of Rome; for the first Christians in the imperial city, the blood of these two premier Apostles made them the founders of a new, Christian Rome. The zealous persecutor of the Church and the chosen leader who denied his Master attest to the victory of God's love over our sins and failings. They are the two Apostles who are most familiar to us; they emerge in the pages of the Gospels and Epistles as flesh-and-blood figures. The rest of the Twelve follow in their wake and take their places now, as they once did around the table at the Last Supper. Apart from legend, we know very little about them. But we do know from Scripture that they are the bedrock of the New Jerusalem: "And the wall of the city had twelve foundations, and on them the twelve names of the twelve apostles of the Lamb" (Rev 21:14). And, as we look back to the apostolic foundation of the Church, we also look ahead to the wedding feast of the Lamb at the end of time. Then the Apostles, who in this life went their separate ways to bear witness to Christ "to the end of the earth" (Acts 1:8), will be gathered together again. Jesus himself promised them this at the Last Supper: "You are those who have continued with me in my trials; as my Father appointed, a kingdom for me, so do I appoint for you that you may eat and drink at my table in my kingdom, and sit on thrones judging the twelve tribes of Israel" (Lk 22:28–30). As we picture the Apostles as a group during our celebration, we see in their reunion a foretaste of the heavenly banquet.

Next the Canon names twelve martyrs, saints who either died in Rome or who were special favorites of the Roman people when the Eucharistic Prayer was composed. First come the three immediate successors of Saint Peter, Linus, Cletus, and Clement; about the first two we know little, but Clement was the author of a celebrated letter from the Church of Rome to the Corinthian Christians, written around the year 95. In that letter, Clement provides the earliest extant testimony to the martyrdom of Peter and Paul: "Let us take the noble examples furnished in our own generation. Through envy and jealousy, the greatest and most righteous pillars have been persecuted and put to death. Let us set before our eyes the illustrious apostles. Peter, . . . when he had at length suffered martyrdom, departed to the place of glory due to him. Owing to envy, Paul also obtained the reward of patient endurance . . . and suffered martyrdom under the prefects."[1] Sixtus is probably the second pope of that name, martyred in the year 258. The Canon violates its usual pattern of listing the saints in chronological order by placing Cornelius (d. 253) after Sixtus, to link his name with that of the celebrated North African bishop and martyr Saint Cyprian of Carthage. Cornelius and Cyprian were a great support to one another at a time when the Church was wracked by persecution from without and schism from within, and they have been honored on the same date (September 16) since the fourth century.

Two other ministers are named after these six bishops: Lawrence the deacon and Chrysogonus, who is traditionally thought to have been in holy orders. Little is known of Chrysogonus, but Lawrence was, after Peter and Paul, the favorite martyr among the Romans. He served as deacon to Sixtus II and was renowned for his charity.

[1] *Letter to the Corinthians*, 5, in Alexander Roberts and James Donaldson, eds., *Ante-Nicene Fathers*, vol. 1, *The Apostolic Fathers, Justin Martyr, Irenaeus* rev. ed. (1885; reprinted, Peabody, Mass.: Hendrickson, 1995), 6.

With the Prayers of the Saints

The procession ends with four laymen: John and Paul, who were venerated in a church built on the Caelian Hill in the fourth century, and Cosmas and Damian, who in fact were Eastern martyrs, famous not only for the testimony of their lives but because as doctors they accepted no payment for treating the sick. Devotion to them in Rome emerged in the sixth century, so they were probably among the last saints to be added to the Canon. In fact the roll-call was not sacrosanct, and it was not uncommon to find one or two other saints added to the list in various places.

What are we, at the beginning of the third millennium, to make of this list of ancient and often unfamiliar figures? As a concession to the sense of ennui some seem to feel in the face of this litany of names, the priest can omit most of them—which is a pity. It is true that many of them are little more than names (this is true of the Apostles as well as the martyrs), but the catalogue of names itself conjures up the impression of a gathering of many saints, an assembly in which no one is simply a face in the crowd, a cipher without individual identity. Let us recall one of the characteristics of the Good Shepherd: "He calls his own sheep by name and leads them out" (Jn 10:3). These saints appeared in the infancy of the Church's life, and they act as a hinge connecting all subsequent history to the apostolic age. As martyrs they bore witness to the saving Blood of the Lamb by pouring out their own blood, so their mention in the Eucharistic sacrifice is most appropriate. Finally, they are representative of diverse human types and varied patterns of sanctity. Man and woman, fisherman and scholar, zealot and tax collector, aristocrat and peasant, layman and priest, doctor and deacon—the very lack of precise information about many of them underscores the one quality that unites these people of differing abilities, temperaments, and personalities: wholehearted faith in Christ.[2]

That they are only representative is indicated by the words *and all your Saints*: our communion includes all the citizens of heaven, both those who are canonized and the millions of other holy men and women who rejoice around God's throne. The wording as we come to the end of this prayer brings to a close the first section of intercessory prayer, begun right after the *Sanctus*. In that prayer [84] we asked the Father to guard and protect the whole Church; now we ask him to hear the same petition the saints make on our behalf: *we ask that through their merits and prayers, in all things we may be defended by your protecting help.*

And then comes, for the first time, the concluding formula *through Christ our Lord. Amen.* Our prayer for the Church and the saints' prayer for us both ascend to the Father through Christ; there is no alternate route. Jesus himself said so clearly at the Last Supper: "I am the way, and the truth, and the life; no one comes to the Father, but by me" (Jn 14:6). The saints are not in competition with the Lord: it is precisely as members of his Body that they pray for us, just as it is our union in Christ that makes it possible for us to pray for one another. This concluding formula will appear several more times in the Canon, although it is often not said aloud, since some think that it breaks up the unity of the Eucharistic Prayer (which is why it appears in parentheses). Spoken or not, the words serve to remind us that Christ is our one Mediator with the Father: "Through him we have obtained access to this grace in which we stand,

[2] More biographical information about the saints of the Roman Canon is given in the appendix to this book.

and we rejoice in our hope of sharing the glory of God"
(Rom 5:2).

As we conclude our reflections on this prayer, we should
note another feature of it that shows how in the Catholic
liturgy the veneration of the saints is integrally united to the
paschal mystery of Christ. This part of the Roman Canon
includes variable additions for the major events in the life
of Christ celebrated throughout the liturgical year:

On the Nativity of the Lord
and throughout the Octave

Celebrating the most sacred night (day)
when blessed Mary the immaculate Virgin
brought forth the Savior for this world,
and in communion with those whose memory we
  venerate . . .

On the Epiphany of the Lord

Celebrating the most sacred day
on which your Only Begotten Son,
eternal with you in your glory,
appeared in a human body, truly sharing our flesh,
and in communion with those whose memory we
  venerate . . .

From the Mass of the Paschal Vigil
until the Second Sunday of Easter

Celebrating the most sacred night (day)
of the Resurrection of our Lord Jesus Christ in the flesh,
and in communion with those whose memory we
  venerate . . .

In Memory of Me

On the Ascension of the Lord

Celebrating the most sacred day
on which your Only Begotten Son, our Lord,
placed at the right hand of your glory
our weak human nature,
which he had united to himself,
and in communion with those whose memory we
  venerate . . .

On Pentecost Sunday

Celebrating the most sacred day of Pentecost,
on which the Holy Spirit
appeared to the Apostles in tongues of fire,
and in communion with those whose memory we
  venerate . . .

In communion with those whose memory we venerate. . . .
The Eucharist is the sacred meal in which the memory of
Christ's death and Resurrection becomes so vivid that they
become a reality in our midst. Our personal "memory" of
the paschal mystery is received from those who, both by
word and example, handed it on to us. It is this "shared
memory" that constitutes the communion of the Body of
Christ, the Church. In proclaiming the roll-call of the ancient heroes of our faith, we follow the example of the Letter to the Hebrews, whose entire eleventh chapter is given
over to remembering great examples of faith in the Old Testament—Abel, Noah, Abraham and Sarah, Moses, and the
rest. The Letter to the Hebrews goes on to paint a picture
of the communion of saints that expresses beautifully what
happens in our Eucharistic celebration:

76

Therefore, since we are surrounded by so great a cloud of witnesses, let us also lay aside every weight, and sin which clings so closely, and let us run with perseverance the race that is set before us, looking to Jesus the pioneer and perfecter of our faith, who for the joy that was set before him endured the cross, despising the shame, and is seated at the right hand of the throne of God. (Heb 12:1−2)

VI

He Has Delivered Us from
the Dominion of Darkness
(Colossians 1:13)

87. Therefore, Lord, we pray: graciously accept this oblation of our service, that of your whole family; order our
days in your peace, and command that we be delivered from
eternal damnation and counted among the flock of those
you have chosen. (Through Christ our Lord. Amen.)

87. Hanc ígitur oblatiónem servitútis nostrae, sed et cunctae fam-
íliae tuae, quaesumus, Dómine, ut placátus accípias: diésque nos-
tros in tua pace dispónas, atque ab aetérna damnatióne nos éripi
et in electórum tuórum iúbeas grege numerári. (Per Christum
Dóminum nostrum. Amen.)

We are approaching the heart of the Eucharistic Prayer, but
before taking that step we pause to join the particular intentions of this congregation to the offering about to be made
on the altar. The function of this prayer is akin to what happens at Mass during the "Prayer of the Faithful", or Intercessions, that conclude the Liturgy of the Word.[1] Prayers are
offered for general intentions (the needs of the Church and

---

[1] The Second Vatican Council (SC, no. 53) directed that the General Intercessions (also known as "The Prayer of the Faithful" because
in ancient times the intercessions were made after the catechumens had
been dismissed) be restored to the Roman liturgy. These intercessions

the world, those who are suffering in some way, the local community), and then the people may be invited to pray in silence for their particular intentions, or (if circumstances allow) voice them aloud.

It seems that before the time of Gregory the Great this prayer in the Canon took many forms, to suit different circumstances. Perhaps tensions arose when intentions were omitted or the challenge of doing justice to the number of particular intentions grew too onerous; whatever the cause, Saint Gregory determined that, apart from a few special occasions, mention should be made at this point of only two overarching desires: peace here and eternal life hereafter. The special occasions were celebrations like baptism, ordination, marriage, or religious profession, when prayers would be offered for those entering into a new role in the life of the Church. For example, here is the prayer offered at Easter for the newly baptized:

> Therefore, Lord, we pray:
> graciously accept this oblation of our service,
> that of your whole family,
> which we make to you
> also for those to whom you have been pleased to give
> the new birth of water and the Holy Spirit,
> granting them forgiveness of all their sins:
> order our days in your peace,
> and command that we be delivered from eternal
>   damnation
> and counted among the flock of those you have chosen.

---

at the end of the Liturgy of the Word had disappeared because many of the intentions came to be included in the Canon and in a litany at the beginning of Mass; they were preserved only in the Good Friday liturgy.

He Has Delivered Us

As part of the liturgical reform undertaken in the wake of the Second Vatican Council, the *Roman Missal* has restored the special texts of this prayer for the dedication of a church, the elect prior to baptism, and at ordinations, weddings, the blessing of an abbot/abbess, and religious profession.

The offering to which our intentions are attached is made by the officiating clergy (*our service*) and the people as well (*that of your whole family*). Our plea to the Father for our earthly needs is simple: *Order our days in your peace*! When we think of the circumstances in which Gregory the Great lived, we can understand why this intention would be foremost in his mind. When he ascended to the Chair of Peter in the year 590, the Italian peninsula had been wracked by barbarian invasions for over 150 years. The civil administration of the empire in the West had collapsed; warfare was incessant, bringing in its wake the twin scourges of famine and plague; the population of Rome, which had been over a million in the second century, had dropped to less than 100,000. It is hard to picture what it must have been like to live in Rome at the end of the sixth century, but if we think of the images we see of human suffering and degradation in war-torn parts of our modern world and then try to imagine such afflictions stretching back over a century, with no relief in sight, we can gain some understanding of why the pope added this prayer for peace to the Canon. How to bring about peace between warring peoples? Gregory believed that this could only be accomplished in the same way Christ had first brought about peace between Jew and Gentile:

> For he is our peace, who has made us both one, and has broken down the dividing wall of hostility, by abolishing

> in his flesh the law of commandments and ordinances, that he might create in himself one new man in place of the two, so making peace, and might reconcile us both to God in one body through the cross, thereby bringing the hostility to an end. And he came and preached peace to you who were far off and peace to those who were near; for through him we both have access in one Spirit to the Father. (Eph 2:14–18)

Gregory also knew that the cruelty and misery afflicting his people were manifestations of a state of affairs that marred the whole of creation and that this, too, could find its remedy only in Christ's sacrifice: "For in him all the fulness of God was pleased to dwell, and through him to reconcile to himself all things, whether on earth or in heaven, making peace by the blood of his cross" (Col 1:19–20).

Why can true peace come only through the Blood of Christ? The discord in our world was born from a primordial revolt that put the human race at enmity with God. Here we meet a biblical truth that is uncongenial and often ignored: the wrath of God. In many religious traditions, and certainly throughout the Old Testament, the offering of sacrifice has been associated with *propitiation*. Something is wrong and must be put right; an offering is made to express sorrow for sin, and the victim represents the offerer's gift of himself to God. To speak of God being "offended" or "angry" is to use woefully anthropological language, but it is the only language available for us to express a rupture in personal relationships.

One of the themes running through the New Testament is that Christ, by his self-offering on the Cross, has atoned for all human sin and reconciled us to God. As we read in the First Letter of John, "He is the expiation for our sins, and not for ours only but also for the sins of the whole world" (1 Jn 2:2). This is our expiatory offering *to* God, because Jesus is truly our brother and can act on behalf of the human race; but it is also an expiatory offering *from* God, because the Father sent his Son into the world precisely to reconcile us to himself. Saint Paul teaches: "[S]ince all have sinned and fall short of the glory of God, they are justified by his grace as a gift, through the redemption which is in Christ Jesus, whom God put forward as an expiation by his blood, to be received by faith" (Rom 3:23–25). And later he writes, "Since, therefore, we are now justified by his blood, much more shall we be saved by him from the wrath of God" (Rom 5:9).

Christ's sacrifice was propitiatory, and since the Eucharist is Christ's sacrifice, our Eucharistic offering is propitiatory, too. Jesus himself linked the idea of propitiation with the Eucharist at the Last Supper: "Drink of it, all of you; for this is my blood of the covenant, which is poured out for many for the forgiveness of sins" (Mt 26:27–28). To be sure, this propitiation was accomplished once and for all on the Cross, as the Letter to the Hebrews explicitly teaches (9:11–10:18). But it is necessary for us to draw on the merits of that sacrifice continually, which is why the Lord taught us to pray daily, "forgive us our trespasses". We must be reconciled to the Father before the channels of grace can be opened to us; in truth, reconciliation and sanctification are two sides of the same coin, and propitiation and petition are intimately connected. This prayer alludes to Christ's atonement by our asking that the Father *graciously accept* our oblation. The Latin reads, *placátus accípias*—literally (but awkwardly), "now that you have been appeased, may you accept". In our daily following of Christ, and especially when we celebrate the

Eucharist, we are doing what the Letter to the Hebrews invites us to do: "Therefore, brethren, since we have confidence to enter the sanctuary by the blood of Jesus, by the new and living way which he opened for us through the curtain, that is, through his flesh, and since we have a great priest over the house of God, let us draw near with a true heart in full assurance of faith, with our hearts sprinkled clean from an evil conscience and our bodies washed with pure water" (Heb 10:19–22). We have confidence to draw near because of Christ's atoning sacrifice, which continually reconciles us to the Father, thereby opening for us the springs of divine grace.

So, when we ask God to order our days in his peace, we affirm that the root of all human dissension and strife is alienation from God and that "peacemaking" will not be accomplished by treaties or troops, important as these might be. Discord is a spiritual problem, and it calls for a spiritual solution. As we pray in the Third Eucharistic Prayer: "May this Sacrifice of our reconciliation . . . advance the peace and salvation of all the world." Within the communion of the Church, it is appropriate for us to intercede particularly for those assuming a new role within the community (the elect, the newly baptized, clergy, married couples, and religious) by joining our petition to the sacrifice of propitiation, as the Letter to the Hebrews urges: "Let us then with confidence draw near to the throne of grace, that we may receive mercy and find grace to help in time of need" (Heb 4:16).

The second petition raises our thoughts again from this world to the world to come. Two very different ideas coalesce: on the one hand, the communion of saints, so vividly recalled in the previous prayer; on the other hand, the awareness of the eternal consequences if God's offer of reconcili-

ation is refused. And so we pray: *Command that we be deliv-*
ered from eternal damnation and counted among the flock of those
you have chosen. The word of God continually encourages us
to be confident but warns us not to be presumptuous. We
should be confident because God desires all people to be
saved (I Tim 2:4), and he "has not destined us for wrath,
but to obtain salvation through our Lord Jesus Christ, who
died for us so that whether we wake or sleep we might live
with him" (I Thess 5:9–10). We should not be presumptuous because "God is not mocked, for whatever a man sows,
that he will also reap. For he who sows to his own flesh
will from the flesh reap corruption; but he who sows to
the Spirit will from the Spirit reap eternal life" (Gal 6:7–8).
We pray to be *counted among the flock of those you have chosen*;
because Jesus himself has warned us that at the Judgment
he will separate his sheep from the goats, and to the latter
he will say: "Depart from me, you cursed, into the eternal
fire prepared for the dèvil and his angels" (Mt 25:41).

As we see the violence and discord that plague our world,
we call to mind that in the Eucharist we are associated with
the heavenly liturgy in which we draw near "to Jesus, the
mediator of a new covenant, and to the sprinkled blood
that speaks more graciously than the blood of Abel" (Heb
12:24). The Blood of Jesus cries out for reconciliation, not
vengeance. But we do well to heed the sober warning that
follows: "See that you do not refuse him who is speaking. For if they did not escape when they refused him who
warned them on earth, much less shall we escape if we reject
him who warns from heaven" (Heb 12:25).

VII

It Is Time for the Lord to Act

(Psalm 119:26)

88. Be pleased, O God, we pray, to bless, acknowledge, and approve this offering in every respect; make it spiritual and acceptable, so that it may become for us the Body and Blood of your most beloved Son, our Lord Jesus Christ.

88. Quam oblatiónem tu, Deus, in ómnibus, quaesumus, bene-díctam, adscríptam, ratam, rationábilem, acceptabilémque fácere dignéris: ut nobis Corpus et Sanguis fiat dilectíssimi Fílii tui, Dómini nostri Iesu Christi.

One the most dramatic events in the Old Testament is the contest between the prophet Elijah and the priests of Baal on Mount Carmel. Elijah challenged them to a duel: he and they would each prepare a bull for sacrifice; they would call upon Baal, and he upon the Lord: "And the God who answers by fire, he is God" (1 Kings 18:24). The priests of Baal performed a dramatic ritual, whipping themselves into a frenzy, to no avail. Elijah in his turn built an altar of twelve stones and placed his bull upon it and, to emphasize his confidence in God, had the sacrifice doused with water. In answer to Elijah's prayer, "Then the fire of the LORD fell, and consumed the burnt offering, and the wood, and the stones, and the dust, and licked up the water that was in the trench. And when all the people saw it, they fell on their faces;

and they said, 'The LORD, he is God; the LORD, he is God'"
(1 Kings 18:38–39).

Like Elijah, we have completed our preparations; we have
done all that can humanly be done. This prayer is a plea that
the Lord will accept our offering and perfect it in such a way
that it becomes the Body and Blood of Christ. How profoundly it is connected with the Institution Narrative that
follows, in which our request is answered, is suggested by
the fact that in the Latin, the entire description of what Jesus
did at the Last Supper is a relative clause appended to this
prayer. It has been called the upbeat before the full measure
of the Institution Narrative.

In this prayer we ask God to transform our gifts. Here we
need to consider briefly what might seem to be a rather the-
oretical question: Does the Roman Canon have an epiclesis?
In the *Catechism of the Catholic Church* we read: "The *Epiclesis*
('invocation upon') is the intercession in which the priest
begs the Father to send the Holy Spirit, the Sanctifier, so
that the offerings may become the body and blood of Christ
and that the faithful, by receiving them, may themselves become a living offering to God [cf. *Rom* 12:1]" (CCC 1105).
The next paragraph of the *Catechism* says that the epiclesis is
at the heart of the Eucharistic celebration, so the question
is not a fine point, of concern only to liturgical historians.
This is an ecumenical issue as well, since the tradition of
the East is that the invocation of the Holy Spirit effects the
transformation of the gifts.

The question of the epiclesis in the Roman Canon has
greatly exercised the attention of scholars, but a book intended for spiritual reflection need not walk down all the
avenues they have traversed. In its earliest form, it seems
that the epiclesis was simply a prayer asking God to trans-

form the gifts, without specifying Father, Son, and/or Holy
Spirit. For example, toward the end of the second century,
Saint Irenaeus wrote: "Bread, . . . when it receives the invocation of God is no longer common bread, but the Eucharist."[1] As trinitarian theology developed, the change was
sometimes attributed to the agency of the Logos (the Word
through whom God creates) or to the Spirit (the source of
sanctification). By the end of the fourth century, orthodox
theology was emphasizing the fully personal identity of the
Holy Spirit in the mystery of the Trinity, and this encouraged greater attention to the role of the Spirit in the work
of salvation. In Syria initially and then throughout the East,
the consecration was attributed to the action of the Holy
Spirit. In the West, however, it has always been associated
with the words of Christ.[2] In the Roman Canon the prayer
for the transformation of the bread and wine into Christ's
Body and Blood is addressed to the Father, but there is a subtle allusion to the involvement of the Logos and the Holy
Spirit in bringing this about, as we shall see in a moment.

We ask God to make our offering *in every respect*, that
is, thoroughly and perfectly, several things: *benedíctam, adscríptam, ratam, rationábilem, acceptabilémque*. At first glance,
the terms seem to have a legal, contractual ring to them.

---

[1] *Against Heresies* 4, 18, 5, in Alexander Roberts and James Donaldson, eds., *Ante-Nicene Fathers*, vol. 1, *The Apostolic Fathers, Justin Martyr,
Irenaeus*, rev. ed. (1885; reprinted, Peabody, Mass.: Hendrickson, 1995),
486.

[2] We should be careful not to exaggerate this difference. Western Fathers who spoke of the efficacy of the words of institution also spoke of
the sanctifying power of the Holy Spirit in the Eucharist, and Eastern
Fathers who spoke of the consecratory effect of the epiclesis also spoke
of the efficacy of the words of institution. More importantly, the three
Persons of the Trinity never act in isolation from one another.

Roman culture had a genius for law, so in one sense these words might be construed as synonymous adjectives describing a sacrifice that is "in order". But in fact at root these are biblical terms, and some reflection on their origin enriches our understanding of what we are asking for in this prayer.

The first adjective, *benedíctam*, seems to be straightforward enough: that our oblation will be blessed. But we must remember that, when Jesus blessed the bread and wine at the Last Supper, he gave them a new reality: "This is my Body. . . . This is my Blood." The second adjective is *adscríptam*: written down, or recorded; the English renders this as *acknowledged*. In official terms, the oblation is duly "registered"; but the biblical allusion is to the book of life, which records all those who are dedicated to God: "He who conquers shall be clothed like them in white garments, and I will not blot his name out of the book of life; I will confess his name before my Father and before his angels" (Rev 3:5; see also Rev 13:8; 21:27). Then, *ratam*: our offering is ratified or completely valid. The Letter to the Hebrews speaks of Christ's sacrifice in these terms: "Hence even the first covenant was not ratified without blood. . . . Thus it was necessary for the copies of the heavenly things to be purified with these rites, but the heavenly things themselves with better sacrifices than these. For Christ has entered, not into a sanctuary made with hands, a copy of the true one, but into heaven itself, now to appear in the presence of God on our behalf" (Heb 9:18; 23–24). To ask that our offering be ratified is to ask that it be united to Christ's one perfect sacrifice.

The final two qualities have an even richer biblical pedigree. In the Old Testament, for an offering to be *acceptable*, the victim had to be free of defects: "And when any one offers a sacrifice of peace offerings to the LORD . . . from the herd or from the flock, to be accepted it must be perfect; there shall be no blemish in it" (Lev 22:21). But there is also an emphasis on the inner state of the one making the offering ("The sacrifice acceptable to God is a broken spirit; a broken and contrite heart, O God, you will not despise" Ps 51:17), and the Lord often rebuked Israel through her prophets for the disparity between their scrupulous performance of sacrificial rites and the immorality in their lives. In the New Testament, our sacrifice is acceptable because it is offered to the Father through Christ: "[B]e yourselves built into a spiritual house, to be a holy priesthood, to offer spiritual sacrifices acceptable to God through Jesus Christ" (1 Pet 2:5). But here, too, we find a demand that our offering be ratified in our lives. Saint Paul urges the Romans: "I appeal to you therefore, brethren, by the mercies of God, to present your bodies as a living sacrifice, holy and acceptable to God, which is your spiritual worship" (Rom 12:1). There can be no doubt that, insofar as what we offer is Christ's sacrifice, it is acceptable, because he is the Lamb without blemish. But as we offer ourselves with him, then our sacrifice is acceptable to the extent that we configure ourselves to Christ. In effect, we are asking God not only to transform the bread and wine into Christ's Body and Blood, but to transform us as well, as Saint Paul himself goes on to say: "Do not be conformed to this world but be transformed by the renewal of your mind, that you may prove what is the will of God, what is good and acceptable and perfect" (Rom 12:2).

The final adjective to consider is *rationábilem*. Literally, the Latin word means "rational" or "reasonable" and at its simplest merely refers to an immaterial, spiritual offering as opposed to blood sacrifices. The word translates the Greek *logikon*, so the association with reason alludes to "the Word" and points up a distinctive feature of Christ's sacrifice: unlike animals, who do not understand what is happening to them, Jesus intentionally gave his life to redeem us. "For this reason the Father loves me, because I lay down my life, that I may take it again. No one takes it from me, but I lay it down of my own accord" (Jn 10:17–18). The word *logikon* appears twice in the New Testament. The first time is in the passage we just saw from the Letter to the Romans about offering our bodies as a living sacrifice, "which is your *spiritual* worship". The other appearance is in the First Letter of Saint Peter: "Like newborn infants, long for the pure *spiritual* milk" (1 Pet 2:2). The fact that the word *rationabilis* can be rendered either "reasonable" or "spiritual" suggests a connection with the Word and the Spirit: in asking the Father to make our offering *rationábilem*, we imply the participation of Christ and the Holy Spirit in transforming our gifts into the Body and Blood of Christ. And we ask that the gift of ourselves may also engage our wills so that, like Christ, we may intend wholeheartedly to give ourselves to God.

The Father's acceptance makes our offering the Body and Blood of Christ *for us*. The Lord's presence is dynamic, not static: he is present as our offering, in which our sacrifice is taken up and completed. Our sacrifice is united to his: "Through him then let us continually offer up a sacrifice of praise to God, that is, the fruit of lips that acknowledge his name" (Heb 13:15). But he is also *for us* as the model of generous love and as the means for us to imitate that model: we want the offering to become for us what it is in itself, the Body and Blood of the one who poured himself out for love of us and who enables us to do the same for one another. Thus the Letter to the Hebrews goes on to say: "Do not neglect to do good and to share what you have, for such sacrifices are pleasing to God" (Heb 13:16).

The Roman Canon uses a simple but evocative word to speak of this "becoming": *fiat*. At the very beginning of the Bible we read: "The earth was without form and void, and darkness was upon the face of the deep; and the Spirit of God was moving over the face of the waters. And God said, 'Let there be light' [*fiat lux*]; and there was light" (Gen 1:2–3). The Spirit of God hovers, the word is spoken, and creation comes into being. Similarly, at the beginning of the New Testament, Mary is told by the angel: "The Holy Spirit will come upon you, and the power of the Most High will over-shadow you; therefore the child to be born will be called holy, the Son of God" (Lk 1:35). She responds, "[L]et it be to me [*fiat mihi*] according to your word" (Lk 1:38). Finally, in the Garden after the Last Supper, Jesus asked the Father to take the cup of suffering away, but he added, "neverthe-less, not as I will, but as you will [*fiat voluntas tua*]" (Mt 26:39). The great mysteries of our faith—creation, Incarna-tion, redemption—all unfold according to the Father's will, as he speaks his Word and the sanctifying Spirit descends. The Father's power is at work now in the Eucharist, a new creation in which the same Christ who was conceived in Mary's womb becomes present through the transformation of our gifts, and his saving sacrifice is offered up in our midst.

God's word is all-powerful, but his omnipotence stops at the threshold of our freedom. He invites our participation in his Son's self-offering, and the divine *fiat* needs to be an-swered by our personal consent, the *fiat mihi* of Mary, the *fiat voluntas tua* of Jesus in Gethsemane, the daily prayer of the Christian, "Thy will be done." The bread and wine are material offerings, and they do not resist God's word. We, on the contrary, can: the intention, the consent that makes our self-offering rational and spiritual, can be withheld or mitigated. We pray that the gifts transformed into the Body and Blood of Christ will strengthen us as ". . . we all attain to the unity of the faith and of the knowledge of the Son of God, to mature manhood, to the measure of the stature of the fulness of Christ" (Eph 4:13).

There is one final biblical allusion to note in this prayer: *your most beloved Son, our Lord Jesus Christ.* The set of prayers that began after the Preface by addressing our *most merciful Father* concludes by speaking of his *most beloved Son.* This affectionate title calls to mind two central events in the life of Jesus. The first was his baptism: "And when Jesus was baptized, he went up immediately from the water, and behold, the heavens were opened and he saw the Spirit of God descending like a dove, and alighting on him; and behold, a voice from heaven, saying, 'This is my beloved Son, with whom I am well pleased'" (Mt 3:16–17). The second was the occasion when Jesus took Peter, James, and John up onto a high mountain: "And he was transfigured before them, and his face shone like the sun, and his garments became white as light. . . . [A] bright cloud overshadowed them, and a voice from the cloud said, 'This is my beloved Son, with whom I am well pleased; listen to him'" (Mt 17:2, 5). As the priest says the words that proclaim the Father's infinitely tender love for his Son, his hands rest over the gifts like a hovering dove or an overshadowing cloud —if not an invocation, certainly an evocation of the Holy Spirit. In the next prayer, Jesus himself will speak through the lips of his priest, and fire will descend from heaven.

VIII

O Taste and See
That the Lord Is Good!

(Psalm 34:8)

89. On the day before he was to suffer, he took bread in his holy and venerable hands, and with eyes raised to heaven to you, O God, his almighty Father, giving you thanks he said the blessing, broke the bread and gave it to his disciples, saying:

TAKE THIS, ALL OF YOU, AND EAT OF IT,
FOR THIS IS MY BODY,
WHICH WILL BE GIVEN UP FOR YOU.

90. In a similar way, when supper was ended, he took this precious chalice in his holy and venerable hands, and once more giving you thanks, he said the blessing and gave the chalice to his disciples, saying:

TAKE THIS, ALL OF YOU, AND DRINK FROM IT,
FOR THIS IS THE CHALICE OF MY BLOOD,
THE BLOOD OF THE NEW AND ETERNAL COVENANT,
WHICH WILL BE POURED OUT FOR YOU AND FOR MANY
FOR THE FORGIVENESS OF SINS.

DO THIS IN MEMORY OF ME.

89. *Qui, prídie quam paterétur, accépit panem in sanctas ac venerábiles manus suas, et elevátis óculis in caelum ad te Deum Patrem suum omnipoténtem, tibi grátias agens benedíxit, fregit, dedítque discípulis suis, dicens:*

In Memory of Me

ACCÍPITE ET MANDUCÁTE EX HOC OMNES:
HOC EST ENIM CORPUS MEUM,
QUOD PRO VOBIS TRADÉTUR.

90. *Símili modo, postquam cenátum est, accípiens et hunc prae-*
clárum cálicem in sanctas ac venerábiles manus suas, item tibi
grátias agens benedíxit, dedítque discípulis suis, dicens:

ACCÍPITE ET BÍBITE EX EO OMNES:
HIC EST ENIM CALIX SÁNGUINIS MEI
NOVI ET AETÉRNI TESTAMÉNTI,
QUI PRO VOBIS ET PRO MULTIS EFFUNDÉTUR
IN REMISSIÓNEM PECCATÓRUM.

HOC FÁCITE IN MEAM COMMEMORATIÓNEM.

This is the jewel for which the whole Eucharistic Prayer is
the setting: we are at table with Jesus and the Twelve for the
Last Supper. The atmosphere surrounding these direct and
simple phrases seems quite different from what has come before; it is almost reportorial. We must remind ourselves that
this is a prayer: we are still addressing God the Father through
Christ our Lord, who *on the day before he was to suffer. . . .*
The Institution Narrative is at the heart of nearly all of the
ancient Eucharistic liturgies. It enjoys a special prominence
in the West, because of our belief that the consecration takes
place when the words of Christ are spoken. This tradition is
very venerable, going back through the Latin Fathers at least
as far as Saint Ambrose. Even earlier, in the second century,
Saint Justin Martyr had written: "For not as common bread
and common drink do we receive these; but in like manner as Jesus Christ our Savior . . . had both flesh and blood
for our salvation, so likewise have we been taught that the
food which is blessed by the prayer of His word, and from
which our blood and flesh by transmutation are nourished,

is the flesh and blood of that Jesus who was made flesh."[1] However, this does not mean that the rest of the Eucharistic Prayer is unimportant or superfluous. Early in the twentieth century the eminent liturgical historian Adrian Fortescue neatly expressed the relationship of the Institution Narrative to the rest of the Eucharistic Prayer in this way: The Roman Canon is one prayer, and the consecration is the answer to that one prayer; the transformation takes place at the Institution Narrative but is the effect of the whole prayer.

There are four accounts of the institution of the Eucharist in the New Testament: those given by Matthew and Mark are similar, and those in Luke's Gospel and Paul's First Letter to the Corinthians are like one another but vary somewhat from Matthew and Mark. (Recall that Saint Luke was a companion of Saint Paul.) The Institution Narratives in all the ancient liturgies draw on these biblical accounts, but they combine them and include details not mentioned in the New Testament. It may well be that the liturgical texts preserve traditions that are older than the brief accounts preserved in the Bible, since the community's celebration of the Eucharist predates those accounts. During the early centuries, the wording of the Institution Narratives in the Eucharistic liturgy was influenced by three factors: 1. A desire to give sym-

---

[1] *First Apology* 66, 1 in Alexander Roberts and James Donaldson, eds., *Ante-Nicene Fathers*, vol. 1, *The Apostolic Fathers, Justin Martyr, Irenaeus*, rev. ed. (1885; reprinted, Peabody, Mass.: Hendrickson, 1995), 185. This understanding was not unknown in the East, either: Saint John Chrysostom speaks of the transformation of the gifts being brought about by the words of Christ. However, it should be noted that whether they attributed the change to words of Christ or the invocation of the Holy Spirit, the Fathers were concerned to stress the real presence of Christ's Body and Blood in the Eucharist, not the precise moment when the transformation took place.

metry to the consecration of the bread and wine; 2. A reliance on the biblical accounts; 3. The need for additional words to express reverence and reflect the meaning of what Christ said and did at the Last Supper. The Scriptures should not be divorced from the community in which they were written: the accounts of the Last Supper found in the venerable liturgical texts exemplify the symbiotic relationship between the written word of God and the living tradition of the Church.

The following schema shows the parallels in the consecration of the bread and wine:

On the day before he was to suffer	In a similar way, when supper was ended,
he took bread in his holy and venerable hands, and with eyes raised to heaven to you, O God, his almighty Father, giving you thanks	he took this precious chalice in his holy and venerable hands,
	and once more giving you thanks,
he said the blessing, broke the bread and gave it to his disciples, saying:	he said the blessing and gave the chalice to his disciples, saying:
TAKE THIS, ALL OF YOU, AND EAT OF IT, FOR THIS IS MY BODY,	TAKE THIS, ALL OF YOU, AND DRINK FROM IT, FOR THIS IS THE CHALICE OF MY BLOOD, THE BLOOD OF THE NEW AND ETERNAL COVENANT,
WHICH WILL BE GIVEN UP FOR YOU.	WHICH WILL BE POURED OUT FOR YOU AND FOR MANY FOR THE FORGIVENESS OF SINS. DO THIS IN MEMORY OF ME.

O Taste and See That the Lord Is Good!

We will now consider the Narrative line by line. The Canon introduces the account of the Last Supper with the words: *On the day before he was to suffer.* The Eastern Eucharistic Prayers generally set the stage with some variation of Saint Paul's words, "On the night when he was betrayed" (1 Cor 11:23), as do our Second and Third Eucharistic Prayers. (Eucharistic Prayer IV uses words inspired by the Gospel of John: "For when the hour had come for him to be glorified by you, Father most holy, having loved his own who were in the world, he loved them to the end".) The Roman Canon links the Last Supper with Christ's death, but it may be that the reference to betrayal created uneasiness, especially for a community so intimately connected with Peter, the Apostle who had denied his Master. The memory of Peter's failure remained fresh in the consciousness of the Roman Church, and the scene of Christ, Peter, and the rooster was depicted on the walls of the catacombs. During the early centuries of persecution, bishops in some places held that Christians who had denied the faith could not be reconciled with the Church, but the popes urged that those who had apostatized under pressure and later repented should be welcomed back. The memory of Peter's fall, and the experience of the frailty of Christians in times of persecution, made it clear to the Romans that Jesus had not been betrayed by Judas alone; as we enter the Upper Room, we all come as poor sinners.

Some words added to this prayer on Holy Thursday remind us that Christ freely embraced his Passion out of love for us and underscore the immediacy of the events that took place at the Last Supper: *On the day before he was to suffer for our salvation and the salvation of all, that is today.* . . . In a sense, every Mass is that "today", and we should bear in mind that everything that took place in the Upper Room is part of our celebration: the gift of the Eucharist, the Lord's washing of his disciples' feet, his farewell discourse, and his final prayer. From time to time we might prayerfully read through the Holy Thursday account in Saint John's Gospel, especially in the presence of the Blessed Sacrament, to deepen our appreciation for the meaning of the Eucharist.

He took bread in his holy and venerable hands: these reverential words, repeated later concerning the chalice, invite us to recall how often in the Gospels Christ acted through the medium of his hands. With those *holy and venerable hands* he healed the sick, blessed children, shared out the loaves and fishes, and reached out to Peter when he began to sink; on Good Friday, they were pierced with nails, and at Easter their scarred palms were proof that he who had been crucified was truly alive again. Those same hands are eternally lifted up in heaven to intercede for us.

And with eyes raised to heaven to you, O God, his almighty Father: the biblical accounts do not describe Jesus raising his eyes to heaven at this time, but there are three other occasions when we are told he did this, and they enrich our understanding of what is happening at table. The first time was at the multiplication of the loaves and fishes: "Taking the five loaves and the two fish he looked up to heaven, and blessed, and broke and gave the loaves to the disciples, and the disciples gave them to the crowds" (Mt 14:19). The similarity between the description of this miracle and that of the Last Supper is deliberate. God had fed the Israelites in the wilderness with manna through the hand of Moses; that providential gift had planted the seed of a promise that God himself would feed his people (see Ezek 34:11−16 and Is 25:6); that promise was fulfilled when God literally fed his people with his own hand in the multiplication of the loaves and fishes. That wondrous feeding, the only miracle recounted in all four Gospels, pointed ahead to a still more wondrous gift: God would give the food, and God would *be* the food. "I am the living bread which came down from heaven; if any one eats of this bread, he will live for ever; and the bread which I shall give for the life of the world is my flesh" (Jn 6:51). The Eucharist as the medicine of immortality is suggested by the second occasion when Jesus raised his eyes and spoke to his Father—at the tomb of Lazarus, just before he summoned him from death to life (Jn 11:41). The third and final occasion was at the end of the Last Supper itself, when Jesus asked the Father to glorify him and to share his glory with his disciples, the *com-panions* who shared his bread. Toward the end of that prayer, he asked, "Father, I desire that they also, whom you have given me, may be with me where I am" (Jn 17:24). The mention of the simple gesture of Jesus' raising his eyes to heaven evokes a chain of providential works, each containing the promise of a greater gift still: God gives his people food and drink in the desert through Moses; God feeds them in person with loaves and fishes; God gives himself as food in the Eucharist; and the Eucharist itself anticipates the heavenly banquet that will never end.

The narrative continues: "*giving you thanks he said the blessing. . . .*" This wording combines two different biblical traditions: Matthew and Mark say that Jesus "took bread, and blessed, and broke it" (Mt 26:26; Mk 14:22); Luke and Paul say he "took bread, and when he had given thanks he broke it" (Lk 22:19; 1 Cor 11:24). In a Jewish meal, the celebration began when the father broke the bread and shared it among those at table, saying: "Blessed are you, Lord our God, King of the universe, who brings forth bread from the earth." Our "blessing" is addressed primarily to God, whom we acknowledge as the source of all we have, so it is equivalent to "giving thanks". Every blessing refers back to God as the source of all good and reaches its fulfillment as an expression of praise: persons and objects are blessed to the extent that they embody the goodness bestowed by their Creator, and in this way they glorify God. The whole sweep of the Eucharistic Prayer, from its initial invitation, "Let us give thanks to the Lord our God" to its concluding doxology is captured in the few simple words, *giving you thanks he said the blessing.*

Jesus *broke the bread and gave it to his disciples.* This action was a part of the Jewish meal ritual, and it expressed the bond uniting those gathered at table. As Saint Paul reminded the Corinthians, "Because there is one bread, we who are many are one body, for we all partake of the one bread" (1 Cor 10:17). "The breaking of the bread" is the oldest name for the Eucharistic celebration; this expression does not appear in either Jewish or classical literature, but it is used three times in the Acts of the Apostles (2:42, 46; 20:7). Saint Luke also employs this term in the account of the appearance of the risen Christ to the disciples on the road to Emmaus: "Then they told what had happened on the road, and how he was known to them in the breaking of the bread" (Lk 24:35). So, although the gesture was not novel, it is clear that for the first Christians it had taken on a new and very profound significance, which we will consider when we see what Jesus said when he gave the bread to his disciples. The "today" connecting the community gathered around the altar to the disciples at table in the Upper Room is expressed by the fact that throughout the Institution Narrative the priest not only says what Christ said, but does what Christ did (even, in the Roman Canon, raising his eyes to heaven)—but he does not break the bread until just before the people come forward to receive Holy Communion. In this way, the fraction rite takes on a solemnity of its own, being both a symbolic and a practical gesture. In the Roman Rite, the bond of unity among believers in the Eucharist is heightened by the exchange of the Kiss of Peace just before the breaking of the bread, whereas in all other Eucharistic liturgies this takes place at the end of the Liturgy of the Word.

When he gave the bread to his disciples, Jesus said: "*Take this, all of you, and eat of it, for this is my Body, which will be given up for you.*" In the beginning, God spoke and all things were made; at Cana, Jesus changed water into wine. In the great miracle of the new creation, at the wedding feast of the Lamb, Jesus changes bread into his Body. The second half of the sentence expresses Jesus' intention to lay down his life for us, and the phrase has an interesting history. It was in an early form of the Roman Canon (Saint Ambrose cites it), but sometime between the fourth and the seventh century it was removed; it has been restored since the Second Vatican Council. Although not found in Matthew and Mark, the words "which is given for you" appear in some versions of Luke's Institution Narrative, and in Paul's account some versions read "this is my Body which is [broken] for you." It is impossible to resolve the discrepancies between these biblical texts, but what is beyond doubt is that the words express Jesus' intention to lay down his life for us; that the first Christians believed that he freely died for our salvation; and that Jesus associated what he did at the Last Supper with what he would do on Calvary. Christ's intention is evident from the fact that he freely chose to go to Jerusalem even though he knew he would be killed there, and in his own words he gave the meaning he attached to his death: "For the Son of man also came not to be served but to serve, and to give his life as a ransom for many" (Mk 10:45). As to the understanding of the first Christians, the idea that Christ has brought about our salvation by his death runs all through the New Testament. The Letter to the Hebrews expresses succinctly and explicitly that his Body is given for us: "We have been sanctified through the offering of the body of Jesus Christ once for all" (Heb 10:10). Jesus "hands himself over" as food to the disciples in the Upper Room just as he will "hand himself over" to death for them later that night. There is also an echo of the inner life of the Trinity here—the Son's very being is relational. When he says "This is my Body", it is always *for you*: for us, but also for the Father and the Spirit. The offering of the body of Jesus Christ just spoken of in the Letter to the Hebrews was carried out because the Son said to the Father, "Behold, I have come to do your will" (Heb 10:9). And it was carried out in obedience to the Spirit, who led him from the beginning of his ministry (see Lk 4:1, 18), and "through the eternal Spirit [Christ] offered himself without blemish to God" (Heb 9:14).

This quality of "being-for-others" was manifested above all on the Cross, but it is the hallmark of Jesus' whole existence. The Letter to the Hebrews speaks of Christ offering himself once for all on the Cross, but it traces that selflessness to the very beginning of his life:

> Consequently, when Christ came into the world, he said,
>
> > "Sacrifices and offerings you have not desired,
> > but a body have you prepared for me;
> > in burnt offerings and sin offerings you have
> > taken no pleasure.
> > Then I said, 'Behold, I have come to do your will,
> > O God,'

as it is written of me in the roll of the book."
(Heb 10:5–7)

The Body given in the Eucharist is not just the Body on
the Cross: the whole history of that Body is contained in
the gift. The Body we receive in Holy Communion was
conceived in Mary's womb, grew to manhood, walked the
roads of Palestine, felt hunger and thirst, wrought great mir-
acles, was nailed to the tree, rose from the dead, and now
reigns in heaven. This truth is beautifully expressed in the
fourteenth-century hymn *Ave verum*, which was often sung
in the Middle Ages at the elevation of the Host:

> Hail true Body, born of the Virgin Mary!
> Who truly suffered and was sacrificed on the
>   Cross for mankind,
> From whose pierced side Blood truly streamed!
> Be for us a foretaste of heaven in our final agony,
> O gentle, kind, and loving Jesus, Mary's Son.

The description of the consecration of the wine parallels
the consecration of the bread in many ways, but the sacrificial motif is more explicit, both in the biblical accounts and
in the Canon. The most solemn moment of the Jewish ritual
came at the end of meal, when the father took a cup filled
with wine and a little water, pronounced a series of blessings, and then all present drank from it. This was known as
"the cup of blessing", and it is to this that Saint Paul refers
when he asks, "The cup of blessing which we bless, is it not
a participation in the blood of Christ?" (1 Cor 10:16). Blood
was at the heart of the Jewish religion—the blood of the
paschal lamb protecting the Israelites at Passover, the rites
carried out by Moses to seal the covenant between God and
his people through the sprinkling of blood, the thousands of

animals whose blood was shed in sacrifice, even the kosher laws calling for all the blood to be removed from meat before it could be eaten. The ninth chapter of the Letter to the Hebrews deals extensively with the theme of how all the blood sacrifices of the old covenant have been fulfilled and surpassed by the Blood of Christ: "For if the sprinkling of defiled persons with the blood of goats and bulls and with the ashes of a heifer sanctifies for the purification of the flesh, how much more shall the blood of Christ, who through the eternal Spirit offered himself without blemish to God, purify your conscience from dead works to serve the living God" (Heb 9:13–14). The saving power of Christ's Blood is spoken of often in the New Testament: by it we are redeemed (1 Pet 1:19; Eph 1:7); we are freed from our sins (Rev 1:5, 7:14); through this Blood we are able to draw near to God (Eph 2:13) and find peace (Col 1:20).

He took this precious chalice: the connection between the Last Supper and the Mass is suggested by the identification of *this* chalice the priest is holding with the one held by Jesus. Why *precious* [*praeclárum*]? This is not only a reverential term (like *holy and venerable hands*); it is also an allusion to the Latin Vulgate translation of a line in Psalm 23 (22): "*calix meus inebrians, quam præclarus est!*" (My chalice that inebriates, how admirable it is!) The Vulgate follows the Greek Septuagint in rendering the Hebrew word usually translated "overflowing" as "inebriating", and both Greek and Latin Fathers interpreted this psalm as speaking of sacramental and mystical joy. This connection to a psalm that describes the abundance of the Messianic Banquet ("you lay out a feast for me, you anoint my head with oil, my cup is so full that I feel tipsy") balances the more sober association of the "cup" with Christ's Passion—a meaning Jesus himself will use a few hours later during his Agony in the Garden. Jesus asks each of us the question he put once to some of his disciples: "Are you able to drink the chalice that I am to drink?" (Mt 20:22), a point we will consider in more depth when we reflect on the final words of Jesus in the Institution Narrative. But beyond the Cross, the wedding feast of the Lamb awaits, and the allusion to Psalm 23 speaks of the joy of that banquet.

After he had pronounced the customary Jewish blessing, Jesus gave the chalice to his disciples, saying: "*Take this, all of you, and drink from it, for this is the chalice of my Blood, the Blood of the new and eternal covenant, which will be poured out for you and for many for the forgiveness of sins.*" Our text combines elements from the four biblical accounts. All four have words to the effect that this is "the [new] covenant in my blood", to which the prayer adds the word *eternal.* The source for this is once again the Letter to the Hebrews: "Now may the God of peace who brought again from the dead our Lord Jesus, the great shepherd of the sheep, by the blood of the *eternal covenant*, equip you with everything good that you may do his will, working in you that which is pleasing in his sight, through Jesus Christ; to whom be glory for ever and ever. Amen" (Heb 13:20–21). This exhortation at the end of Hebrews echoes an idea proclaimed at its very beginning: "In many and various ways God spoke of old to our fathers by the prophets; but in these last days he has spoken to us by a Son, whom he appointed the heir of all things, through whom also he created the world" (Heb 1:1). The history of God's people to this point is the chronicle of a series of covenants; now, in Christ, the final and definitive covenant has been made. This Blood will be poured out for you (Lk) and for many (Mt/Mk) for the forgiveness of sins (Mt).

The translation of *pro multis* has been a source of contention ever since those responsible for the earlier English version of the Roman Missal rendered it as "for all [men]"; the new translation is more faithful to both the Latin of the Roman Canon and the Greek of the New Testament. It is certainly true that Christ poured out his life's Blood for all people without exception. This is the faith of the Catholic Church (CCC 605), and it is a truth explicitly taught in the New Testament. But salvation involves our cooperation, and it is noteworthy that the two biblical passages that most clearly enunciate the conviction that Christ died for everyone also speak of our response: "And he died for all, that those who live might live no longer for themselves but for him who for their sake died and was raised" (2 Cor 5:15); "we have an advocate with the Father, Jesus Christ the righteous; and he is the expiation for our sins, and not for ours only but also for the sins of the whole world. And by this we may be sure that we know him, if we keep his commandments" (1 Jn 2:1–3). The covenant in Christ's Blood is new, eternal, and definitive; it includes Gentiles as well as Jews; but it is not automatic, because love always entails freedom, and freedom always entails the ability to reject the other's offer of love.

The "blood of the covenant" would be a familiar idea to Jesus' disciples. After Moses proclaimed God's Law to the Israelites on Mount Sinai and they pledged to obey it, he sacrificed animals and sprinkled some of their blood on the altar. Then, "Moses took the blood and threw it upon the people, and said, 'Behold the blood of the covenant which the LORD has made with you in accordance with all these words'" (Ex 24:8). What would *not* be familiar, and indeed must have shocked the disciples, was the invitation to drink

Christ's Blood. (The notion was especially abhorrent to the Jews, given their laws requiring all blood to be removed from meat before it could be eaten.) Yet Jesus could not have been more explicit: "Truly, truly, I say to you, unless you eat the flesh of the Son of man and drink his blood, you have no life in you; he who eats my flesh and drinks my blood has eternal life, and I will raise him up at the last day. For my flesh is food indeed, and my blood is drink indeed. He who eats my flesh and drinks my blood abides in me, and I in him" (Jn 6:53–56). This is not just poetic language: Saint John tells us that many of Christ's followers found this teaching so offensive that they left him. Jesus did not qualify his words to win them back; he simply asked the Twelve, "Will you also go away?" (Jn 6:67). We should not allow the familiarity of the words at Mass, the solemn gestures and setting, blind us to the audacity of what Christ is doing: he gives us his very Body and Blood. Can he give us anything more?

The final words of Christ are: "*Do this in memory of me.*" This is the second place where our prayer has been altered from the version in use before the Second Vatican Council. Christ's command does not appear in Matthew and Mark, and in Luke the words are associated with the breaking and sharing of bread at the beginning of the meal. In Paul's account, Christ gives the command twice: "[T]he Lord Jesus on the night when he was betrayed took bread, and when he had given thanks, he broke it, and said, 'This is my body which is for you. Do this in remembrance of me.' In the same way also the chalice, after supper, saying, 'This chalice is the new covenant in my blood. Do this, as often as you drink it, in remembrance of me'" (1 Cor 11:23–25). The older wording in the Roman Canon was based on Paul's account but had to be adapted to include the breaking and sharing of the bread: "As often as you do these things, you shall do them in remembrance of me." The revised wording indicates that "this" refers to both the breaking of the bread and the sharing of the cup.

The Greek word for "memorial", *anamnesis*, has great significance in Christian tradition, and we will explore its meaning when we reflect on the prayer that follows the Institution Narrative [92]. At its simplest, the Lord's command is to do what he did at the Last Supper. What is distinctive, however, is not the action (since the breaking of bread and sharing of the cup of blessing were customary Jewish practices), but the meaning or content those actions will have for his followers: "Do this in memory *of me*." The acclamation and prayer that follow the consecration suggest what this new meaning is.

Before moving on to that acclamation and prayer, we might pause to reflect on the deeper challenge contained in Christ's command at the Last Supper. In a few hours he will be arrested, and the next day he will be put to death in a most painful and humiliating way. Jesus goes freely to his death, handing over his Body to be crucified and allowing his Blood to be poured out for love of us. His death is the crowning moment of a life lived in selfless dedication to others. It is the purpose that Christ gives to his approaching death that makes it sacrificial and, thus, the pattern for all authentic discipleship. This, too, is what he means when he says, "*Do this in memory of me*." As majestic as the imagery contained in the Letter to the Hebrews is—Christ the victorious High Priest entering the heavenly Tent bearing the Blood of his sacrifice—the author does not lose sight of the fact that "in the days of his flesh, Jesus offered up prayers and supplications, with loud cries and tears" (Heb 5:7). Nor does he lose sight of its implications for us: "So Jesus also suffered outside the gate in order to sanctify the people through his own blood. Therefore let us go forth to him outside the camp, bearing abuse for him" (Heb 13:12–13).

IX

Great Indeed, We Confess, Is the Mystery of our Religion
(1 Timothy 3:16)

91. The mystery of faith.

We proclaim your Death, O Lord, and profess your Resurrection until you come again.

Or: When we eat this Bread and drink this Cup, we proclaim your Death, O Lord, until you come again.

Or: Save us, Savior of the world, for by your Cross and Resurrection you have set us free.

91. Mystérium fídei.

Mortem tuam annuntiámus, Dómine, et tuam resurrectiónem confitémur, donec vénias.

Vel: *Quotiescúmque manducámus panem hunc et cálicem bíbimus, mortem tuam annuntiámus, Dómine, donec vénias.*

Vel: *Salvátor mundi, salva nos, qui per crucem et resurrectiónem tuam liberásti nos.*

This acclamation following the Institution Narrative is the most significant change made to the Roman Canon after the Second Vatican Council. The older form for the consecration of the wine may be translated: "This is the chalice of my Blood, of the new and eternal testament, the mystery of faith: which shall be shed. . . ." The words *the mystery of faith* do not appear in the biblical accounts of the Last Supper or in any other Eucharistic liturgies or in the early version of the Canon quoted by Saint Ambrose. Over the centuries various explanations have been advanced for their presence in the Roman Canon, but liturgical scholars have no clear understanding of when or why they were interpolated into the Institution Narrative. The decision was made to remove them from the prayer of consecration and use them to introduce an acclamation directed to Christ immediately after the consecration.

Although most of our prayers at Mass are addressed to the Father, there are times when we pray to Christ—for example, the "Lord, have mercy" in the penitential rite and the "Lamb of God" during the fraction rite. This new acclamation addressed to Christ in the Roman Rite has its roots in older traditions. In several of the Eastern Eucharistic Prayers, it is customary for the choir or people to sing "Amen!" after the words "This is my Body" and "This is my Blood." In the West, this acclamation follows in the line of customs adopted since the thirteenth century to add solemnity to the consecration and express adoration of Christ, who is present under the forms of bread and wine: the elevations of the Host and chalice, kneeling by the people, genuflections by the priest. Only faith reveals that Christ is present, so should we understand "the mystery of faith" to refer simply to the real presence of Christ in the Eucharist? If this were so, the acclamation would more appropriately be something like, "My Lord and my God"; but the mystery here, while including the transformation of the elements, refers to something more far-reaching. The biblical origin of the phrase points us to this wider vista.

Great Indeed Is the Mystery of Our Religion

In the First Letter to Timothy, Paul lists this among the qualities to be looked for in deacons: "They must hold the mystery of the faith with a clear conscience" (1 Tim 3:9). A few verses on, he suggests what is meant by this "mystery of faith":

> Great indeed, we confess, is the mystery of our religion:
>
> > He was manifested in the flesh,
> > vindicated in the Spirit,
> >   seen by angels,
> > preached among the nations,
> > believed on in the world,
> >   taken up in glory. (1 Tim 3:16)

Given the prayer we are considering, it is interesting that this description takes the form of an acclamation (many biblical scholars believe that the Letter is quoting a hymn); the "mystery" embraces Christ's whole life: his Incarnation, victory over death, and glorification. Saint Paul uses the word "mystery" elsewhere to refer to specific things: Christ living in us (Col 1:27), the inclusion of the Gentiles in the People of God (Eph 3:6), the bond of husband and wife as an expression of the love between Christ and his Church (Eph 5:32), our bodily resurrection (1 Cor 15:51). More fundamentally, the "mystery" is Christ himself: "For I want you to know how greatly I strive . . . for all who have not seen my face, that their hearts may be encouraged as they are knit together in love, to have all the riches of assured understanding and the knowledge of God's mystery, of Christ, in whom are hidden all the treasures of wisdom and knowledge" (Col 2:1–3).

The *mystery of faith* does refer to the presence of Christ in the Eucharist; this is evident from the fact that the acclamation is addressed to him. But Christ is not present as an object, like the relic of a saint; he is the living Christ, present in person, Body and Blood, soul and divinity. This is why the Eucharist contains and reveals to the eyes of faith the whole economy of salvation, the paschal mystery of Christ born, crucified, and risen.

As to the wording of the acclamations themselves, they are inspired in part by what Saint Paul wrote immediately after his account of the Institution Narrative: "For as often as you eat this bread and drink the chalice, you proclaim the Lord's death until he comes" (1 Cor 11:26). We proclaim the Lord's death, because he himself identified the bread and wine with his Body given over to death and his Blood poured out in sacrifice. But we do not simply look back to that event two thousand years ago: the living, risen Christ is present now in our midst, and this sacred meal is the foretaste and anticipation of the wedding feast of the Lamb, when Christ returns in glory.

X

I Remembered God,
and Was Delighted

(Psalm 76:4, Vulgate)

92. Therefore, O Lord, as we celebrate the memorial of the blessed Passion, the Resurrection from the dead, and the glorious Ascension into heaven of Christ, your Son, our Lord, we, your servants and your holy people, offer to your glorious majesty from the gifts that you have given us, this pure victim, this holy victim, this spotless victim, the holy Bread of eternal life and the Chalice of everlasting salvation.

92. Unde et mémores, Dómine, nos servi tui, sed et plebs tua sancta, eiúsdem Christi, Fílii tui, Dómini nostri, tam beátae passiónis, necnon et ab ínferis resurrectiónis, sed et in caelos gloriósae ascensiónis: offérimus praeclárae maiestáti tuae de tuis donis ac datis hóstiam puram, hóstiam sanctam, hóstiam immaculátam, Panem sanctum vitae aetérnae et Cálicem salútis perpétuae.

In his farewell discourse at the end of the Last Supper, Jesus promised that he would ask the Father to send the Spirit of truth to his disciples. "These things I have spoken to you, while I am still with you. But the Counselor, the Holy Spirit, whom the Father will send in my name, he will teach you all things, and bring to your remembrance all that I have said to you" (Jn 14:25–26). The Holy Spirit stirs up our memory of Christ in a unique way during the celebration of the Eucharist. In the Liturgy of the Word, we are reminded of the great works of God, and, following the Lord's directive, we celebrate the Liturgy of the Eucharist in memory of him. The *Catechism of the Catholic Church* says: "The Eucharist is the memorial of Christ's Passover, the making present and the sacramental offering of his unique sacrifice, in the liturgy of the Church which is his Body. In all the Eucharistic Prayers we find after the words of institution a prayer called the *anamnesis* or memorial" (CCC 1362). How do we understand Christ's Passover to be made present in the liturgy, and what is the connection between this and our sacramental offering of his unique sacrifice?

The Jewish celebration of Passover is not merely the commemoration of an event in Israel's past; in some way, the events of the Exodus become present (see CCC 1363). A clue as to how this can be so is found in the third blessing at the end of the meal for feast days, a prayer also used to consecrate Temple sacrifices: in it, God is asked to "remember" Jerusalem, the Messiah, and the whole Jewish people, with mercy and goodness. The God who intervened to free his people from slavery continues to "remember" them, and this creates a mysterious permanence to his saving deeds on their behalf. God's people are celebrating God's fidelity: first, to himself and his covenant and, then, to them. They in turn "remember" what he has done, and is doing, for them and give thanks (and offer sacrifice) to pledge their faithfulness to God in return. Their expression of fidelity is rooted in God's fidelity to them. When Jesus said, "*Do this in memory of me*" at the end of the Last Supper, he was using language that already had a religious meaning to his Jewish disciples.

His association of those words with his Body to be given over and his Blood to be shed gave the words a new meaning.

The Christian Passover, the definitive act of God's saving mercy, is Christ's redemptive death and Resurrection. Jesus "was put to death for our trespasses and raised for our justification" (Rom 4:25). Christ's glorification is the sign that his sacrifice has been accepted by the Father. This is why *we celebrate the memorial of the blessed Passion, the Resurrection from the dead, and the glorious Ascension into heaven of Christ, your Son, our Lord*. Christ's Passion is *blessed* (the Latin *tam beátae* is more emphatic: *exceedingly blessed*) because it is the source of our salvation. Christ's Ascension is *glorious* because it represents his victory over the realm of death:

> Therefore it is said,
>
>> "When he ascended on high he led a host of captives,
>> and he gave gifts to men."
>
> (In saying, "He ascended," what does it mean but that he had also descended into the lower parts of the earth? He who descended is he who also ascended far above all the heavens, that he might fill all things.) (Eph 4:8–10)

The paschal mystery of Christ's death and Resurrection is made present in our midst by our fulfillment of Christ's command to "remember" him in the Jewish sense: not as someone who died two thousand years ago, but as the living presence of God's fidelity now.

Because we "remember" Christ's Passion, Resurrection, and Ascension, we, *your servants and your holy people* (that is, clergy and laity together), offer sacrifice in thanksgiving to the Father. This part of the Canon has been called the most explicitly sacrificial prayer in the entire Mass, and we need to ask what this language means. Certainly it does *not* mean that we are offering some sacrifice independent of Christ's sacrifice on the Cross. The Letter to the Hebrews is explicit: "But when Christ had offered for all time a single sacrifice for sins, he sat down at the right hand of God, then to wait until his enemies should be made a stool for his feet. For by a single offering he has perfected for all time those who are sanctified" (Heb 10:12–14). But our ability to offer sacrifice comes from our union with Christ: as the members of his Body, we can make our offering together with his. Subjectively, our sacrifice means imitating Christ's selfless love and total adherence to his Father's will. Saint Paul exhorted the Corinthians to do just this: "For Christ, our Paschal Lamb, has been sacrificed. Let us, therefore, celebrate the festival, not with the old leaven, the leaven of malice and evil, but with the unleavened bread of sincerity and truth" (1 Cor 5:7–8).

But there is an objective element in our sacrifice, too, which does not depend on the degree of our individual sincerity and truth: Christ's own sacrifice is present on the altar as the great sign of God's fidelity to his people, and we unite our imperfect, limited offerings to his infinite and perfect one. The Canon adopts a reverential tone, speaking of our offering being made *to your glorious majesty*; the very intimacy of the gift of his Son increases our sense of awe in the Father's presence. And we frankly own that we are like small children buying a present for our mother, because anything we have to offer is first of all God's gift to us. So, we offer *from the gifts that you have given us*, as David said long ago: "But who am I, and what is my people, that we should be able thus to offer willingly? For all things come from you, and of your own have we given you" (1 Chron

29:14). This is true of the offering any creatures make to their Creator, but it is especially true of the Eucharist, because here it is Christ's own sacrifice we offer to the Father. What we offer is nothing less than *the holy Bread of eternal life and the Chalice of everlasting salvation*. We offer what Wisdom first offers us: "With the bread of life and understanding, she shall feed him, and give him the water of wholesome wisdom to drink" (Sir 15:3 [Vulgate]). The "chalice of salvation" we lift up (Ps 116:13) is the Blood of Christ, who is "the power of God and the wisdom of God" (1 Cor 1:24); the bread we offer is Christ himself, who said: "I am the bread of life" (Jn 6:35).

Saint Paul teaches that we offer Christ's own sacrifice: "The cup of blessing which we bless, is it not a participation in the blood of Christ? The bread which we break, is it not a participation in the body of Christ?" (1 Cor 10:16). This is why the Canon dares to apply the word *hostia* (a term that literally means a living creature offered in sacrifice) to the apparently inanimate objects of bread and a chalice: it is the living Christ himself and his sacrifice that are present. The adjectives used to describe this offering emphasize that it is Christ's sacrifice that we offer: *this pure victim, this holy victim, this spotless victim*. But he is not sacrificed again. Catholic teaching is very clear that our Eucharistic sacrifice is the same sacrifice Christ offered on Calvary, which he now offers in an unbloody manner (see CCC 1367).

We return to the teaching of the *Catechism*: the Eucharist is the making present and sacramental offering of Christ and his sacrifice. These twin mysteries—the real presence of Christ in the Eucharist, and the Mass as a sacrifice—are not the result of an effort of imagination on our part, by which we try so hard to picture the biblical events that it is "as if" we are in the Upper Room or on Calvary. Nor are they brought about by some magical power the priest has to change bread and wine simply by uttering some special formula. No, these blessings are a sheer grace, accomplished in our midst by God's fidelity. More fundamental than our "remembering" Christ is God's "remembering" us: he loves us so much that he does not want his Son's life and death to be some distant memory of long ago, of which we learn by hearsay, but to be a reality that touches our lives *now* and so becomes our personal memory. Encountering Christ himself in the Eucharist, we can say what the Samaritans said long ago to the woman at the well: "It is no longer because of your words that we believe, for we have heard for ourselves, and we know that this is indeed the Savior of the world" (Jn 4:42).

Our "remembering" Jesus is grounded in God's "remembering" us, an idea rooted in the Jewish experience of Passover: it is God's "remembering" of his people that transforms the celebration from a merely historical commemoration of the Exodus into a here-and-now event; and so it is with the Eucharist. The word "remember" appears nearly two hundred times in the Old Testament. It usually refers either to exhorting the people to remember their covenant with God or to asking God to remember Abraham and his descendents, and the covenant he has made with them, and so to come to their aid. This theme finds a final expression at the beginning of the New Testament, on the lips of a man who might be said to embody the whole of the Old Testament: Zechariah, the father of John the Baptist. In his canticle of praise at the birth of his son, Zechariah gives thanks that God is about to accomplish his work of redemption through Jesus. He singles out the two characteristic qualities manifested by God when he entered into covenants with his people: mercy and fidelity. "Blessed be the Lord God of Israel, for he has visited and redeemed his people . . . to perform the *mercy* promised to our fathers, and to *remember* his holy covenant" (Lk 1:68, 72). That same mercy and fidelity are at the heart of the mystery of the Eucharist.

As we come to the end of this reflection, we can see how celebrating the Eucharist in memory of Christ is rooted in his "remembering" us. Repeatedly throughout the Old Testament the people begged God to remember them, but there is only one occasion in the New Testament when someone asked Jesus to do this. The incident bespeaks both the petitioner's ability to see through the visible appearances to the underlying reality (as we must with the Blessed Sacrament) and the power inherent in Christ's "remembering". One of the criminals, gazing on the crushed and humiliated victim hanging on the Cross next to him, said, " 'Jesus, remember me when you come in your kingly power.' And he said to him, 'Truly, I say to you, today you will be with me in Paradise' " (Lk 23:42–43).

XI

He Has Regarded the Low Estate of His Handmaiden

(Luke 1:48)

93. Be pleased to look upon these offerings with a serene and kindly countenance, and to accept them, as once you were pleased to accept the gifts of your servant Abel the just, the sacrifice of Abraham, our father in faith, and the offering of your high priest Melchizedek, a holy sacrifice, a spotless victim.

93. Supra quae propítio ac seréno vultu respícere dignéris: et accépta habére, sícuti accépta habére dignátus es múnera púeri tui iusti Abel, et sacrifícium Patriárchae nostri Abrahae, et quod tibi óbtulit summus sacérdos tuus Melchísedech, sanctum sacrifícium, immaculátam hóstiam.

It is audacious for us to associate our offering with Jesus' sacrifice. This prayer and the next recognize this and humbly entreat God to accept our gifts. They might be seen as a pair —in the first, we ask God to look down favorably upon our sacrifice, and in the second we ask him to take it up into his presence—but we will treat them separately.

Here we ask God *to look upon these offerings with a serene and kindly countenance.* The imagery appears several times in Scripture; for example, the Psalmist asks:

> May God be gracious to us and bless us
> and make his face to shine upon us. (Ps 67:1)

This petition is derived from the priestly blessing ordained by God in the Book of Numbers:

> The LORD said to Moses, "Say to Aaron and his sons, Thus you shall bless the sons of Israel: you shall say to them,
> The LORD bless you and keep you:
> The LORD make his face to shine upon you, and be gracious to you:
> The LORD lift up his countenance upon you, and give you peace." (Num 6:22–26)

Why should God look favorably upon our offering and accept it? The prayer recalls the example of three great "offerers" in the Old Testament: Abel, Abraham, and Melchizedek. We appreciate their importance when we reflect on their relationship to Christ and their meaning for us.

The Canon describes Abel as *just*, a virtue attributed to him by Jesus himself. The context where he does this is relevant to the point we are considering here. Our Lord is taking his adversaries to task for their hypocrisy, and he concludes with these words: "Therefore I send you prophets and wise men and scribes, some of whom you will kill and crucify, and some you will scourge in your synagogues and persecute from town to town, that upon you may come all the righteous blood shed on earth, from the blood of innocent [Vulgate: *iusti*] Abel to the blood of Zechariah the son of Barachiah, whom you murdered between the sanctuary and the altar. Truly, I say to you, all this will come upon this generation" (Mt 23:34–36). Christ associates his approaching death with the violent murders of the righteous all the way back to Abel. But he also speaks of those whom he will send, his disciples, who after his death will themselves be driven from town to town, persecuted, and crucified. All innocent blood, both before and after Calvary, is taken up into Christ's sacrifice.

The hostility directed against Jesus was heightened by his words concerning Abraham. When his enemies claimed that Abraham was their father, Christ retorted, "If you were Abraham's children, you would do what Abraham did, but now you seek to kill me, a man who has told you the truth which I heard from God; this is not what Abraham did" (Jn 8:39–40). The argument became more heated, and his opponents accused Jesus of claiming to be greater than Abraham. Jesus said he would not glorify himself, but added: " 'Your father Abraham rejoiced that he was to see my day; he saw it and was glad.' The Jews then said to him, 'You are not yet fifty years old, and have you seen Abraham?' Jesus said to them, 'Truly, truly, I say to you, before Abraham was, I am.' So they took up stones to throw at him; but Jesus hid himself, and went out of the temple" (Jn 8:56–59).

Jesus never mentions the mysterious figure of Melchizedek, who appears only twice in the Old Testament, in chapter 14 of Genesis and in Psalm 110. But he does cite this psalm in reference to himself, again in the context of a controversy. He asked the Pharisees whose son the Messiah is, and they answered, "David's." Jesus responded:

"How is it then that David, inspired by the Spirit, calls him Lord, saying,

'The Lord said to my Lord,
Sit at my right hand,
till I put your enemies under your feet'?

If David thus calls him Lord, how is he his son?" And

no one was able to answer him a word, nor from that day did any one dare to ask him any more questions. (Mt 22:43–46)

When we reflect on the relationship of Abel, Abraham, and Melchizedek to Jesus himself, we find that they are each mentioned or alluded to in the context of the opposition and hostility that will lead to Jesus' death. The conflicts swirl around Christ's identity and his claims, which, if untrue, would indeed be blasphemous: that he is completely innocent and the embodiment of all the righteous who have been unjustly put to death; that he is greater than Abraham and existed before him; and that he is not merely the son of David, but the Son of God. It is in the Letter to the Hebrews that the implications of Jesus' identity for his sacrifice are developed. Melchizedek is presented as a type of Christ for the reasons we have just seen: 1. He is just: "He is first, by translation of his name, king of righteousness" (Heb 7:2). 2. He is greater than Abraham: "This man . . . received tithes from Abraham and blessed him who had the promises. It is beyond dispute that the inferior is blessed by the superior" (Heb 7:6–7). 3. He is like God's Son: "He is without father or mother or genealogy, and has neither beginning of days nor end of life, but resembling the Son of God he continues a priest for ever" (Heb 7:3). The Letter goes on to develop other implications that we have encountered already: that Jesus, the sinless one, freely offered himself, entering the heavenly sanctuary with his own blood, and perfected by a single offering all who are sanctified.

Although these three great figures form part of the sacred history leading to Christ, they are introduced into the Roman Canon more for what they mean for us than for what they tell us about him. We are asking the Father to accept our sacrifice, and, insofar as it is Christ's sacrifice, it has already been accepted. The point of uncertainty is *our* part in the offering and the extent to which we imitate and internalize Christ's self-offering. God's fidelity to us made manifest in the presence and sacrifice of his Son in the Eucharist invites our fidelity in return. These Old Testament heroes are brought forward as models of the inner dispositions with which we should approach God.

Because Melchizedek is such a shadowy figure, there is little to say about the dispositions underlying his sacrifice. What is striking is that he offered bread and wine, the same elements we use in the sacrifice of the Mass. Because food and drink are essential to our existence, we might see in his offering the importance of bringing to the altar all the circumstances of our daily life and affirming the goodness of all God's creation. The words *a holy sacrifice, a spotless victim* were added in reference to Melchizedek's sacrifice by Saint Leo the Great in opposition to the Manicheans, who claimed that wine was evil. There is an antiphon in our Liturgy of the Hours, inspired by the Vulgate translation of 1 Chronicles 29:17, that is fitting here: "With simplicity of heart, I have joyfully offered everything to you, my God" (Second Antiphon, Office of Readings, Saturday, Week 1). When we come into God's presence, we strive to offer him our best, and rightly so; but our lives are made up of shadows as well as lights, and we should cast ourselves as we are into the Lord's arms, trusting that he will increase what is good and heal what is diseased.

Sacred Scripture sheds a little more light on Abel and his sacrifice. We are told in the Book of Genesis: "In the course of time Cain brought to the LORD an offering of the fruit of the ground, and Abel brought some of the firstlings of his flock and of their fat portions. And the LORD had regard for Abel and his offering, but for Cain and his offering he had no regard" (Gen 4:3–5). Why did God look upon Abel's sacrifice *with a serene and kindly countenance*, and not that of Cain? The text does not tell us. It may be that Abel's sacrifice represented a more thorough offering, since it involved the destruction of the firstlings of his flock, rather than just grain, but this is speculation. The New Testament suggests that the reason lies in Abel's inner disposition, not in the sacrifice itself. In answer to the question, "Why did Cain murder Abel?" the First Letter of John answers: "Because his own deeds were evil and his brother's righteous" (1 Jn 3:12). The jealousy in Cain's heart, which would lead him to murder his own brother, tainted the offering he made to God. The Letter to the Hebrews gives another reason: "By faith Abel offered to God a more acceptable sacrifice than Cain, through which he received approval as righteous, God bearing witness by accepting his gifts; he died, but through his faith he is still speaking" (Heb 11:4). The two explanations are in fact complementary: Abel is righteous because of his absolute trust and fidelity to God, and it is from this righteousness that his good actions flow. Cain, on the contrary, performs the external actions of worship, but his heart is far from God.

The fidelity that is willing to sacrifice all for love of God finds a unique expression in the story of Abraham and Isaac. The Canon calls him *Patriárchae nostri*, which the English felicitously translates as *our father in faith*. This rendering is inspired by Saint Paul, who wrote to the Gentile Galatians: "So you see that it is men of faith who are the sons of Abraham" (Gal 3:7). Abraham and Sarah are held up as great models of faith in the Letter to the Hebrews: by faith they left all that was familiar and journeyed to a foreign land; by faith they conceived a child in old age. It then goes on to speak of Abraham's great sacrifice: "By faith Abraham, when he was tested, offered up Isaac, and he who had received the promises was ready to offer up his only-begotten son, of whom it was said, 'Through Isaac shall your descendants be named.' He considered that God was able to raise men even from the dead; hence he did receive him back and this was a symbol" (Heb 11:17–19). For Abraham, God's commandment is heartbreaking. It seems to mean the loss of everything—not only the long-awaited child of his old age, but the fulfillment of all God's promises. Yet he believed that God could even raise the dead and did receive Isaac back. The Greek says he received him back as a parable—as a sign pointing to something else, the Resurrection of Christ. The foundation for Abraham's fidelity is, for Christians, the fidelity of the heavenly Father, who was not only willing to offer up his only Son, but in fact did so; God did not spare his own Son but gave him up for us all (Rom 8:32). Isaac's sacrifice was prevented, but the Son of God really died. His Resurrection represents the recovery of all that seemed irretrievably lost in the Passion. As the sacrifice of the only Son is present on our altar, we are invited to imitate Abraham, our father in faith, and give everything over to God. Saint Paul teaches: "No distrust made him waver concerning the promise of God, but he grew strong in his faith as he gave glory to God, fully convinced that God was able to do what he had promised. That is why his faith was 'reckoned to him as righteousness.'" and "It will be reckoned to us who believe in him that raised from the dead Jesus our Lord, who was put to death for our trespasses and raised for our justification" (Rom 4:20–22, 24–25).

It is a great privilege to unite our offering to Christ's

sacrifice, but it is also costly. We want God to regard us with kindness, but as we stand in the presence of the Cross we remember a daughter of Abraham whom God had regarded favorably in her lowliness. The angel had told her that her child would be called Son of the Most High, that he would reign over the house of Jacob for ever, and of his kingdom there would be no end (Lk 1:32–33). At the end of her Son's short life, she watched him bleed to death on the Cross, gasping in agony. She considered that God was able even to raise men from the dead, and she received him back—not figuratively, but truly. It is with humble faith like Mary's that we should unite our offering to Christ's.

XII

I Brought a Reminder of
Your Prayer Before the Holy One
(Tobit 12:12)

94. In humble prayer we ask you, almighty God: command that these gifts be borne by the hands of your holy Angel to your altar on high in the sight of your divine majesty, so that all of us who through this participation at the altar receive the most holy Body and Blood of your Son may be filled with every grace and heavenly blessing. (Through Christ our Lord. Amen.)

94. Súpplices te rogámus, omnípotens Deus: iube haec perférri per manus sancti Angeli tui in sublíme altáre tuum, in conspéctu divínae maiestátis tuae; ut, quotquot ex hac altáris participatióne sacrosánctum Fílii tui Corpus et Sánguinem sumpsérimus, omni benedictióne caelésti et grátia repleámur. (Per Christum Dóminum nostrum. Amen.)

It is not enough for the Father to look kindly upon our offering—we want him to accept it. The prayer in which we ask for this is inspired by a scene from the Book of Revelation: "And another angel came and stood at the altar with a golden censer; and he was given much incense to mingle with the prayers of all the saints upon the golden altar before the throne; and the smoke of the incense rose with the prayers of the saints from the hand of the angel before God"

(Rev 8:3–4). Angelic presence has been associated with holy places in Scripture as far back as Jacob's dream of the ladder with the angels of God ascending and descending on it (Gen 28:12), and at times in the Old Testament they took part in sacrificial offerings. For example, an angel was present when Samson's father sacrificed a holocaust. "And when the flame went up toward heaven from the altar, the angel of the LORD ascended in the flame of the altar while Manoah and his wife looked on; and they fell on their faces to the ground" (Judg 13:20). They also carried prayers to God, as we read in the Book of Tobit: "I am Raphael, one of the seven holy angels who present the prayers of the saints and enter into the presence of the glory of the Lord" (Tob 12:15). At the very least, this prayer expresses our conviction that the spiritual creation takes part in Christ's oblation and ours; the angels whose voices were heard at the *Sanctus* are still with us.

What is the significance of this altar in heaven mentioned in the Book of Revelation? The Letter to the Hebrews invites further reflection. There we are told that Christ did not enter into the earthly sanctuary, which is only a copy, but into heaven itself. This idea has its origin in an ancient priestly tradition that the Mosaic liturgy with its altar and sacrifices was a copy of heavenly worship: "According to all that I show you concerning the pattern of the tabernacle, and of all its furniture, so you shall make it" (Ex 25:9). The Tent of Meeting, and later the Temple, was the symbolic meeting place between heaven and earth, between God and his people. For Christians, the Temple and its worship are types pointing to Christ, who as God and Man is the true meeting place between heaven and earth. The implications of this are developed in Hebrews and Revelation, but the claim goes back to Jesus himself: "The Jews then said to him, 'What sign have you to show us for doing this?' Jesus answered them, 'Destroy this temple, and in three days I will raise it up.' The Jews then said, 'It has taken forty-six years to build this temple, and will you raise it up in three days?' But he spoke of the temple of his body" (Jn 2:18–21).

At the end of the Book of Revelation we read, "And I saw no temple in the city, for its temple is the Lord God the Almighty and the Lamb" (Rev 21:22). God and the Lamb were introduced earlier in the book, in language reminiscent of the propitiatory throne or "mercy seat" in the Holy of Holies. This is what Moses had constructed according to the pattern he received on Mount Sinai. It consisted of the Ark of the Covenant, over which rested a cover of pure gold flanked by figures of the cherubim; this cover was understood symbolically to be God's resting place. Once a year, on the Day of Atonement, the High Priest entered the Holy of Holies with the blood of the sacrificial lamb. The vision of the heavenly liturgy in the fourth chapter of Revelation describes God seated on a throne, surrounded by the four living creatures and twenty-four elders. Then, "between the throne and the four living creatures and among the elders, I saw a Lamb standing, as though it had been slain" (Rev 5:6). While Revelation describes the Victim, Hebrews speaks of the Priest: in Christ we have a High Priest who can sympathize with our weakness, so "Let us then with confidence draw near to the throne of grace, that we may receive mercy and find grace to help in time of need" (Heb 4:16). Both the Letter to the Hebrews and the Book of Revelation present the relationship between the Jewish sanctuary, Jesus, and heavenly worship in somewhat kaleidoscopic fashion; in later ages, theologians developed systematic and highly imaginative correlations among these realities. The fundamental point to be made here is captured well in one of the Prefaces for the Easter season:

> By the oblation of his Body,
> he brought the sacrifices of old to fulfillment
> in the reality of the Cross
> and, by commending himself to you for our salvation,
> showed himself the Priest, the Altar, and the Lamb of
>   sacrifice.
> (Preface for Easter V)

So, the heavenly altar is Christ himself. When *in humble prayer we ask* that our gift be carried there, what are we requesting? The answer emerges from yet another controversy between Jesus and his adversaries. Jesus is criticizing the casuistry of some Pharisees who make a distinction between binding and non-binding oaths: "And you say, 'If any one swears by the altar, it is nothing; but if any one swears by the gift that is on the altar, he is bound by his oath.' You blind men! For which is greater, the gift or the altar that makes the gift sacred?" (Mt 23:18–19). Jesus the rabbi bases his argument on a teaching found in the Book of Exodus: "[W]hatever touches the altar shall become holy" (Ex 29:37). Our prayer says in a different way what has been said earlier in the Canon: We want to unite our sacrifice to Christ's in such a way that the Father finds it acceptable. Some have suggested that this prayer is a sort of epiclesis, invoking God's power to transform our offering, not by the descent of the Holy Spirit, but by the ascent of the gifts; indeed, some Orthodox theologians at least as far back as Nicholas Cabasilas (d. 1390) have maintained that this *is* the epiclesis in the Roman Canon.

This topic raises complex theological issues that are beyond the scope of this book. For our purposes, it may be helpful to connect the image of the angel bearing our gift to the heavenly altar to the words spoken by Jesus to Nathaniel: "Truly, truly, I say to you, you will see heaven opened, and the angels of God ascending and descending upon the Son of man" (Jn 1:51). The unavoidably spatial terms of "ascending" and "descending" symbolize communion between God and his people, between heaven and earth. In the Old Testament, angels manifested God's presence in such a way that there was a real encounter with him, yet his divine transcendence was safeguarded; their presence was a sign that God had accepted the prayers and sacrifices of his people. In the fullness of time, Christ descended into our world and "through the eternal Spirit offered himself without blemish to God" (Heb 9:14); then he ascended in his glorified humanity to carry that sacrifice before the merciful throne of his Father. Now we pray that our offering may be carried by the hands of angels into the presence of the Father by their contact with the altar in heaven, who is Christ.

The second half of this prayer turns our attention from the splendor of the heavenly liturgy back to ourselves: *so that all of us who through this participation at the altar receive the most holy Body and Blood of your Son may be filled with every grace and heavenly blessing.* Here we diverge from the scene painted in the Book of Revelation. There, "the smoke of the incense rose with the prayers of the saints from the hand of the angel before God" (Rev 8:4); but the saints spoken of in the Apocalypse are those who had been slain for the word of God, and their prayer is for their blood to be avenged (Rev 6:9–10). The answer to that petition is the parousia of final judgment: "Then the angel took the censer and filled it with fire from the altar and threw it on the earth; and there were peals of thunder, loud noises, flashes of lightning, and an earthquake" (Rev 8:5). What we ask for instead, and receive, is a parousia of mercy: our earthly altar and the heavenly altar become one, and as the members of Christ's Body we are sanctified by sharing in his Body and Blood. This prayer looks forward to Holy Communion, when we are guests at the Lord's table. He is our priest, our altar, our sacrifice, and also our sacrificial feast. In his First Letter to the Corinthians, Paul asks: "Consider the people of Israel; are not those who eat the sacrifices partners in the altar?" (1 Cor 10:18); and in the Letter to the Hebrews, we read: "We have an altar from which those who serve the tent have no right to eat" (Heb 13:10). Our *participation at the altar* gives us communion with Christ and communion in Christ.

This communion necessarily entails sharing in Christ's sacrifice: the Letter to the Hebrews goes on to speak of Jesus being driven out of the city to his death and invites us to follow him and share in his rejection. But communion also means a sharing in Christ's triumph, and the conclusion of our prayer alludes to this: *filled with every grace and heavenly blessing.* The words are inspired from a benediction at the beginning of the Letter to the Ephesians: "Blessed be the God and Father of our Lord Jesus Christ, who has blessed us in Christ with every spiritual blessing in the heavenly places" (Eph 1:3). In the following chapter, Paul speaks again of the heavenly places: "But God, who is rich in mercy, out of the great love with which he loved us, even when we were dead through our trespasses, made us alive together with Christ (by grace you have been saved), and raised us up with him, and made us sit with him in the heavenly places in Christ Jesus, that in the coming ages he might show the immeasurable riches of his grace in kindness toward us in Christ

Jesus" (Eph 2:4–7). The grace and blessing for which we pray carries us up once again into the glory of the heavenly liturgy—not just our gifts, but we ourselves are raised up into *the sight of* [*the*] *divine majesty*!

XIII

Blessed Are the Dead
Who Die in the Lord

(Revelation 14:13)

95. Remember also, Lord, your servants N. and N., who have gone before us with the sign of faith and rest in the sleep of peace. Grant them, O Lord, we pray, and all who sleep in Christ, a place of refreshment, light and peace. (Through Christ our Lord. Amen.)

95. Meménto étiam, Dómine, famulórum famularúmque tuárum N. et N., qui nos praecessérunt cum signo fídei, et dórmiunt in somno pacis. Ipsis, Dómine, et ómnibus in Christo quiescéntibus, locum refrigérii, lucis et pacis, ut indúlgeas, deprecámur. (Per Christum Dóminum nostrum. Amen.)

The awareness of our communion with the heavenly court prompts us to call to mind our departed family members and friends. This prayer was originally one of the variable parts of the Roman Canon—it was not used on Sundays or feasts and may have been added ordinarily at a Mass offered for the dead. The language comes to us from the primitive Church; there are literary records of the Eucharist being offered for the deceased as early as the late second century. The Roman Canon is unique in having the *Memento* of the dead separated from the *Memento* of the living. The reason is that we prayed for the living among those who are offering the Eucharistic sacrifice; the dead no longer partake of the sacraments. But they did in this life, and we are consoled by the words of Christ: "[H]e who eats my flesh and drinks my blood has eternal life, and I will raise him up at the last day" (Jn 6:54).

We recall by name those *who have gone before us with the sign of faith and rest in the sleep of peace*. These words carry us back to the age of the catacombs. *Praecessit in pace, praecessit nos in pace, praecessit in somno pacis*, and similar inscriptions appear on early Christian graves. The *sign of faith* is baptism, the sacramental "sealing" of faith, the mark by which Christ stamps those who are his own. The burial places in catacombs and Christian sarcophagi were decorated with biblical scenes alluding to baptism, an expression of our hope for eternal life: "Do you not know that all of us who have been baptized into Christ Jesus were baptized into his death? We were buried therefore with him by baptism into death, so that as Christ was raised from the dead by the glory of the Father, we too might walk in newness of life" (Rom 6:3–4).

We then broaden the horizon of our prayer to include *all who sleep in Christ*. The Church is a sacramental communion, embracing all those marked with the sign of faith in baptism. But God's mercy extends beyond the borders of that communion; others, too, may be saved, but only *in Christ*. They sleep or rest in him; the days of their probation are behind them. In the Book of Revelation, a voice from heaven declares that those who have died in the Lord are blessed: " 'Blessed indeed,' says the Spirit, 'that they may rest from their labors, for their deeds follow them!' " (Rev 14:13).

The faithful departed are blessed, but we pray for them because many need to undergo a final purification as they come into the presence of the all-holy God. We pray that God will grant them *a place of refreshment, light and peace*. The peace and light are those we find at the end of the Book of Revelation, after the travails of the last days: the heavenly Jerusalem, watered by the river of life flowing from the throne of God and the Lamb, a city where it is never night. In a general sense, the word *refrigérii* (*of refreshment*) refers to comfort and happiness in the world to come, as for example the condition of Lazarus in the parable, in contrast to the torments endured by the rich man (Lk 16:19–31). But it also has a particular history. In ancient Rome the word originally meant a libation from which it was believed the dead derived coolness, and it came to mean a funeral feast, including the annual commemorative meal at the grave of the deceased. Many Christians observed this custom, although Church leaders were somewhat ambivalent about it, partly because of its pagan origins and partly because the celebration sometimes got out of hand. We know from the *Martyrdom of Polycarp* that by the middle of the second century a Eucharistic celebration took place on the anniversary of a martyr's death, and over time the Mass became the distinctively Christian version of the *refrigerium*.

There are many depictions in the catacombs of people reclining at table. Art historians offer various interpretations —the elect at the heavenly feast, a celebration of the Eucharist, the *refrigerium*—but in a way these three images meld together. When we gather to celebrate the Eucharist, we experience a foretaste of the wedding feast of the Lamb at which we will be reunited with our loved ones, and by our prayer we give them refreshment as they make their way to that banquet.

In one of the most moving passages in his *Confessions*,

Saint Augustine describes his mother's death. He tells us that previously she had gone to great trouble to arrange to be buried next to her husband; now she was dying at Ostia, hundreds of miles from home. Although Augustine's brother suggested she would be happier dying in her own land, Monica responded: "Bury this body wherever you will; do not be preoccupied about that. All I ask is that you remember me at the altar of the Lord wherever you are" (*Confessions* IX, 11, 27; author's translation). She came to realize that there can be no more lasting monument, no more impressive memorial, for our departed family members and friends than a remembrance at the table of him who said: "I am the living bread which came down from heaven; if any one eats of this bread, he will live for ever; and the bread which I shall give for the life of the world is my flesh" (Jn 6:51).

XIV

According to Your Abundant Compassion, Turn to Me

(Psalm 69:16)

96. To us, also, your servants, who, though sinners, hope in your abundant mercies, graciously grant some share and fellowship with your holy Apostles and Martyrs: with John the Baptist, Stephen, Matthias, Barnabas, (Ignatius, Alexander, Marcellinus, Peter, Felicity, Perpetua, Agatha, Lucy, Agnes, Cecilia, Anastasia) and all your Saints: admit us, we beseech you, into their company, not weighing our merits, but granting us your pardon, through Christ our Lord.

96. Nobis quoque peccatóribus fámulis tuis, de multitúdine miseratiónum tuárum sperántibus, partem áliquam et societátem donáre dignéris cum tuis sanctis Apóstolis et Martyribus: cum Ioánne, Stéphano, Matthía, Bárnaba, (Ignátio, Alexándro, Marcellíno, Petro, Felicitáte, Perpétua, Agatha, Lúcia, Agnéte, Caecília, Anastásia) et ómnibus Sanctis tuis: intra quorum nos consórtium, non aestimátor mériti, sed véniae, quaesumus, largítor admítte. Per Christum Dóminum nostrum.

As with the *Memento* of the living, so again with the dead mention is made of some of the great Apostles and martyrs. But another intention is slipped in—the priests add an appeal for themselves, as poor sinners. The Roman Canon exudes an atmosphere of humility, prompted by awe of God and an awareness of how daring it is for us to associate ourselves with Christ's self-offering. All the more is this true for the priest, who acts *in persona Christi* in the liturgy. The prayer is one of humble self-accusation: we are *servants and sinners* who, *not weighing our merits, hope in* [*God's*] *abundant mercies . . . to* [*grant*] *us . . . pardon*. The sentiments are inspired by the opening words of the *Miserere*, the great psalm of repentance:

> Have mercy on me, O God,
> according to your merciful love;
> according to your abundant mercy blot out
> my transgressions. (Ps 51:1)

While the prayer primarily concerns the officiating clergy, by extension it applies to the whole community; although the Canon distinguishes between priests and people in several places, it never speaks of them in isolation from one another.

We ask that, along with the faithful departed, God will *grant* [*us*] *some share* (*partem áliquam*—some small part) *and fellowship with* [*his*] *holy Apostles and Martyrs* and *admit us . . . into their company*. This is what Paul prayed for as he said farewell to the elders in Ephesus: "And now I commend you to God and to the word of his grace, which is able to build you up and to give you the inheritance among all those who are sanctified" (Acts 20:32). An echo of this prayer appears in the *Letter to the Philippians* written by Saint Polycarp sometime in the first part of the second century: "*det vobis sortem and partem inter sanctos suos*" (May he give you a lot and portion among his holy ones).[1]

---

[1] Although the *Letter to the Philippians* was written in Greek, the complete text survives only in Latin.

As with the saints named earlier in the Canon, the list given here has a definite organizational structure, and it was probably Saint Gregory the Great who gave it its final form. In the first list, the Mother of God led a procession of twenty-four saints, twelve Apostles and twelve martyrs. Here John the Baptist leads a procession of fourteen saints—seven men and seven women. The presence of Mary and John expresses in prayer an image found frequently in Christian art: the *Deesis*, or "Intercession". In many Byzantine churches, we find an icon of Christ in glory, flanked on either side by a row of saints bowing before him in prayerful petition, with Mary and the Baptist standing closest to the Savior on either side. (The theme is not uncommon in Western art, either: in Rome alone, it appears in Cavallini's *Last Judgment* in the church of Saint Cecilia, Raphael's *Disputa* in the Salla della Segnatura, and in Michelangelo's *Last Judgment* in the Sistine Chapel.) One of the oldest surviving examples of this subject is a seventh-century fresco in the church of Santa Maria Antiqua in the Roman forum, painted not long after Gregory gave the list of saints in the Canon their final form.

Saint John the Baptist has been highly venerated from ancient times. His birth is accorded a place on the calendar (an honor shared only with Christ himself and the Mother of God) and is celebrated as a solemnity; there is another feast to commemorate his martyrdom; he was the great Forerunner whose role it was to prepare the way for Christ. The Preface prayed during the Eucharistic Prayer on his feasts expresses well his unique place in the plan of salvation:

> In his Precursor, Saint John the Baptist,
> we praise your great glory,
> for you consecrated him for a singular honor
> among those born of women.

147

His birth brought great rejoicing;
even in the womb he leapt for joy
at the coming of human salvation.
He alone of all the prophets
pointed out the Lamb of redemption.

And to make holy the flowing waters,
he baptized the very author of Baptism
and was privileged to bear him supreme witness
by the shedding of his blood.

It is fitting that he should lead the company of Apostles and martyrs whose companionship we desire.

The first of the seven male witnesses is Stephen, the proto-martyr, whose story is familiar to us from the New Testament. He is followed by two other biblical figures, Matthias and Barnabas. Matthias was the disciple chosen to take the place of Judas; his place among the Apostles earlier in the Canon was taken by Paul, so his name is included here. Barnabas, the companion of Saint Paul, has always been venerated as an Apostle, and a fourth-century document speaks of him preaching the Gospel in Rome. Next comes Ignatius of Antioch, who was martyred in Rome during the reign of Emperor Trajan at the beginning of the second century. There is a tradition that he was ordained by Saint Peter, who lived for a time in Antioch, and he was the author of several letters—including one addressed to the Church at Rome—that tell us a great deal about Christian life at the end of the New Testament age.

Little is known about the rest of the saints, apart from Perpetua. The identity of Alexander is particularly challenging: although he is sometimes identified with Pope Alexander I (105–115), this is unlikely, because there is no early tradition of this bishop suffering martyrdom. Several Roman martyrs had this name, so it is impossible now to know to which of them the Canon refers. An inscription by Pope Damasus claims that he learned of the martyrdom of Marcellinus and Peter from their executioner himself, and later tradition holds that Marcellinus was a priest and Peter an exorcist.

The Canon then lists seven women, of whom the most famous is the African martyr Perpetua. She was put to death on March 7, 202, in Carthage, together with her servant Felicity and several others. Her *Passion* is a contemporaneous account, including a section written by Perpetua herself, so it is among the earliest first-hand accounts of a martyrdom. Because Felicity is mentioned first in the Canon, it is possible that this refers to a Roman martyr of that name, and not to Perpetua's companion. Agatha and Lucy were executed in Sicily. Agnes was a young girl put to death in Rome, and she is the most honored of female martyrs in that city. Devotion to Agnes was very strong from the fourth century on, and Constantine's own daughter built a church over her grave on the Via Nomentana and was buried nearby. Devotion to Cecilia appeared in the fifth century, but the fact that neither Ambrose nor Damasus makes reference to her in the fourth century is rather puzzling. The final woman martyr, Anastasia, was put to death sometime at Sirmium (in Serbia), probably during the Diocletian persecution at the beginning of the fourth century, and her body was brought to Constantinople in the following century; devotion to her spread from there to Rome.

With the exception of the saints mentioned in the New Testament, and Ignatius and Perpetua, little is known of most of the men and women mentioned here in the Canon. The men are organized according to their office, and the women geographically: Africa (Felicity? and Perpetua), Sicily (Agatha and Lucy), Rome (Agnes and Cecilia), the East (Anastasia). They also comprise different stages in life: (the Roman) Felicity, a mother of grown children; Perpetua, a young mother; Cecilia, a bride; Agatha and Lucy, virgins; Agnes, a young girl. These men and women, surrounded by legends and often little more than a name, represent all the unnamed heroes of the first centuries of Christianity—men, women, and children who bore witness to Christ by the shedding of their blood. It has been said that more believers died for the faith in the twentieth century than in all the other centuries put together. In gulags, concentration camps, and killing fields they have borne witness to the Gospel at the cost of their lives; many of their names are unknown to us, and the shadowy figures we invoke from the earliest days of the Christian faith can also symbolize these many witnesses closer to our own day. We may not be called to pay the ultimate price for following Jesus, but true discipleship is costly. As we ask to have some small share in the fellowship of heroic believers, past and present, we make Saint Paul's prayer our own: "May you be strengthened with all power, according to his glorious might, for all endurance and patience with joy, giving thanks to the Father, who has qualified us to share in the inheritance of the saints in light. He has delivered us from the dominion of darkness and transferred us to the kingdom of his beloved Son, in whom we have redemption, the forgiveness of sins" (Col 1:11–14).

XV

In Him All Things Hold Together
(Colossians 1:17)

97. Through whom you continue to make all these good
things, O Lord; you sanctify them, fill them with life, bless
them, and bestow them upon us.

*97. Per quem haec ómnia, Dómine, semper bona creas, sanctíficas,
vivíficas, benedícis, et praestas nobis.*

Our great prayer concludes with two doxologies, one speaking of God's gifts streaming down upon us through Christ,
the other expressing our praise of the Father through the
same Mediator. To understand the meaning of this first
prayer, we must go back to the time before credit cards,
a time when even money was not the principal means of exchange. The "collection" (which is mentioned as far back
as Justin's description of the Mass in the second century)
consisted of the bread and wine for the Eucharist and other
produce intended to provide for the sustenance of the clergy
and the relief of the poor. The bread and wine were solemnly
placed on the altar, and the other gifts were laid nearby.

It was customary on certain occasions to bless some of
these other gifts: for example, water, milk, and honey at baptism, the paschal lamb at Easter, and specific foods on certain saints' days. The practice still survives in the liturgy for
Holy Thursday, when the bishop blesses the Oil for the Sick

at this point in the Eucharistic Prayer. This prayer followed those blessings and expressed gratitude for all the goods of creation, which come to us through Christ. As Paul wrote to the Colossians: "He is the image of the invisible God, the first-born of all creation; for in him all things were created, in heaven and on earth, visible and invisible . . . all things were created through him and for him. He is before all things, and in him all things hold together" (Col 1:15–17).

All these good things includes the Eucharistic gifts but widens to profess our conviction that everything God has made, and which is already good because he has made it, is also somehow sanctified by Christ. Earlier we prayed that God's angel would carry our offering to heaven, and it was as if the ceiling of the church were removed and our earthly celebration were united to the heavenly liturgy. Now it is as if the walls dissolve, and the Eucharistic presence of Christ radiates out to sanctify all creation. The source of this sanctification is the Incarnation; the presence of God in the world as a creature hallows all creation. The ancient "Christmas Proclamation" in the *Roman Martyrology* proclaims that Christ was born in time because he wished to sanctify the world by his gracious coming. That hallowing presence continues in a unique way in the Blessed Sacrament. Through Christ, the Father *sanctifies them, fills them with life, and blesses them* for one reason: to *bestow them upon us*. Every grace, every benefit comes to us from the Father through Christ his Son.

The connection between *all these things* and the Eucharist is made in the New Testament. John begins his account of the Last Supper with these words: "Jesus, knowing that the Father had given all things into his hands, and that he had come from God and was going to God" (Jn 13:3). Paul for his part views God's generosity through the lens of Christ's sacrifice: "He who did not spare his own Son but gave him up for us all, will he not also give us all things with him?" (Rom 8:32). Paul sees this divine generosity as an antidote to the dissension and rivalry that made the Corinthians' Eucharistic celebration such a source of scandal to him: "So let no one boast of men. For all things are yours, whether Paul or Apollos or Cephas or the world or life or death or the present or the future, all are yours; and you are Christ's; and Christ is God's" (1 Cor 3:21–23).

This prayer is therefore an invitation for us to acknowledge gratefully that everything we have is a gift to us from God, who creates good things in order to lavish them upon us. The awareness of this should be an incentive to stewardship: precisely because the bounty of this world *is* God's gift to us, we are to cherish it and not view it as something that exists for us to plunder. If it is true that Christ's presence in the Eucharist sanctifies all creation, it is also true that his presence in us, the members of his Body, should impart to us a spirit of reverence when we handle earthly goods. Reverence and generosity: the pattern of Christ's self-offering, to which we have dared to add our own, is a challenge. A selfless and reverent use of this world's resources is truly Eucharistic, a truth taught long ago by Saint Paul:

> The point is this: he who sows sparingly will also reap sparingly, and he who sows bountifully will also reap bountifully. Each one must do as he has made up his mind, not reluctantly or under compulsion, for God loves a cheerful giver. And God is able to provide you with every blessing in abundance, so that you may always have enough of everything and may provide in abundance for every good work. As it is written,
>
> > "He scatters abroad, he gives to the poor;
> > his righteousness endures for ever."

He who supplies seed to the sower and bread for food will supply and multiply your resources and increase the harvest of your righteousness. You will be enriched in every way for great generosity, which through us will produce thanksgiving to God; for the rendering of this service not only supplies the wants of the saints but also overflows in many thanksgivings to God. (2 Cor 9:6–12)

XVI

We Utter the Amen through Him, to the Glory of God

(2 Corinthians 1:20)

98. Through him, and with him, and in him, O God, almighty Father, in the unity of the Holy Spirit, all glory and honor is yours, for ever and ever. Amen.

98. Per ipsum, et cum ipso, et in ipso, est tibi Deo Patri omnipoténti, in unitáte Spíritus Sancti, omnis honor et glória per ómnia saecula saeculórum. Amen.

"For there is one God, and there is one mediator between God and men, the man Christ Jesus, who gave himself as a ransom for all" (1 Tim 2:5–6). The theme of Christ our Mediator has been a leitmotif running quietly through the whole Roman Canon, and as the prayer comes to its conclusion this idea becomes a dominant note. One prayer after another proclaims it: *through Christ our Lord* [96]; *through whom you continue . . .* [97]; *through him, and with him . . .* [98]. This doxology belongs to the earliest tradition of the Canon and is very similar to a doxology concluding the third-century Eucharistic Prayer of Hippolytus. The wording "through Christ" testifies to its antiquity: it predates the rise of Arianism, which denied the full divinity of the Son. This conflict effected the wording of prayers: orations composed in the wake of the controversy tended to emphasize the equality of the three Persons of the Trinity. For example, the familiar prayer "Glory be to the Father, and to the Son, and to the Holy Spirit" was originally "Glory be to the Father, through the Son, in the Holy Spirit", the pattern followed in this doxology.

Christ is our Mediator, the High Priest who intercedes for us with the Father. But he does not stand in solitary isolation; we pray not only *through* him, but also *with* him and *in* him. We pray *with* him because he is truly our brother, who sympathizes with our weakness because he has become like us in all things but sin. We turn again to that inexhaustible mine, the Letter to the Hebrews:

> For it was fitting that he, for whom and by whom all things exist, in bringing many sons to glory, should make the pioneer of their salvation perfect through suffering. For he who sanctifies and those who are sanctified have all one origin. That is why he is not ashamed to call them brethren, saying,
>
> "I will proclaim your name to my brethren,
> in the midst of the congregation I will praise you."
> And again,
> "I will put my trust in him."
> And again,
> "Here am I, and the children God has given me."
> (Heb 2:10-12)

We pray *in* him because we are members of his Body, the Church. It is the Holy Spirit who unites us to Christ and to one another, which is why Paul exhorts the Ephesians to "maintain the unity of the Spirit in the bond of peace" (Eph 4:3). *In the unity of the Holy Spirit* means the Church, for she is brought into communion and sanctified by the indwelling of the Holy Spirit. The older prayer of Hippolytus makes this connection more explicitly; it concludes: "through your Son Jesus Christ, through whom be to you glory and honor with the Holy Spirit in the holy Church, now and for ever. Amen." If we keep in mind this relationship between the Holy Spirit and the Church, then our concluding doxology is similar to one found in the Letter to the Ephesians: "Now to him who by the power at work within us is able to do far more abundantly than all that we ask or think, to him be glory in the Church and in Christ Jesus to all generations, for ever and ever. Amen" (Eph 3:20–21). *In [Christ]* and *in the unity of the Holy Spirit* view our communion with the Father in relation to Christ, whose Mystical Body we are, and in relation to the Holy Spirit, who vivifies that Body.

What do we offer to the Father? *All glory and honor . . . for ever and ever*, a refrain that occurs several times in the heavenly liturgy described in the Book of Revelation. This is the praise offered by the four living creatures, the twenty-four elders, and myriads of angels to God (Rev 4:9–10; 7:11), or to the Lamb (Rev 5:12), or to both together: "And I heard every creature in heaven and on earth and under the earth and in the sea, and all therein, saying, 'To him who sits upon the throne and to the Lamb be blessing and honor and glory and might for ever and ever!'" (Rev 5:13). Once again, as so often in the Roman Canon, earthly and heavenly worship unite.

There is one seemingly small but important characteristic of our praise to note: we do not pray that *all glory and honor* "may be given" to the Father; we say, *all honor and glory* "is given". As the Church gathers around the altar united in the Holy Spirit and reverently offers Christ's Body and Blood to the Father (symbolized by the priest lifting up the consecrated bread and wine), God actually does receive all glory and honor; the holy sacrifice of the Mass is the highest, the noblest, the most sublime act of public worship. In our Eucharistic celebration, the ancient prophecy of Malachi is fulfilled: "For from the rising of the sun to its setting my name is great among the nations, and in every place incense is offered to my name, and a pure offering; for my name is great among the nations, says the LORD of hosts" (Mal 1:11).

The entire prayer of the Canon ends with what Saint Augustine called "the signature of the people": *Amen*! When the priest began the prayer, he had invited the people to give thanks to the Lord, and they had ratified his invitation with the words: "*It is right and just.*" [83] Now they make their own the great prayer of thanksgiving the priest has proclaimed on their behalf. The importance of this acclamation is clear from the fact that Saint Justin, in the oldest description we have of the Sunday Eucharist (ca. 150), explicitly mentions the "Amen" at the end of the prayer of thanksgiving (see CCC 1345). Saint Jerome reports that the "Amen" reverberated like thunder in the Roman basilicas.

"Amen" is literally the last word in the Bible, too (Rev 22:21). In one word it expresses the mystery of our communion with God in Christ: it is our Yes to the Father and the Father's Yes to us, a Yes sealed by the Holy Spirit himself. As Saint Paul wrote to the Corinthians: "For the Son of God, Jesus Christ, whom we preached among you . . . was not Yes and No; but in him it is always Yes. For all the promises of God find their Yes in him. That is why we utter the Amen through him, to the glory of God. But it is God who establishes us with you in Christ, and has commissioned us; he has put his seal upon us and given us his Spirit in our hearts as a guarantee" (2 Cor 1:19–22). Christ himself is our "Amen" (Rev 3:14): the Father has said everything to us in his Son, and we offer everything to him in return, until the liturgy of heaven and the liturgy on earth are one forever. Concerning the Eucharist, Paul said: "For as often as you eat this bread and drink the chalice, you proclaim the Lord's death until he comes" (1 Cor 11:26). Our final word here below is the final word in Scripture itself: "He who testifies to these things says, 'Surely I am coming soon.' Amen. Come, Lord Jesus! The grace of the Lord Jesus be with all the saints. Amen" (Rev 22:20–21).

APPENDIX

The Saints of the Roman Canon

Among the distinctive elements of the Roman Canon are the two lists of early saints, men and women who bore witness to Christ by the shedding of their blood. A few of them are well known to us, others are just names. In this appendix we will explore their history and how they came to be included in the Canon.

We know from the *Martyrdom of Saint Polycarp* that the practice of venerating the relics of martyrs and celebrating the Eucharist on the anniversary of their death goes back to the middle of the second century in some places. The Christian communities in North Africa had a lively devotion to their martyrs and publicly read the accounts of their deaths on their anniversaries; some of our most reliable records about the martyrs come from that region. It seems that in Rome itself commemoration of the martyrs can be traced back to the middle of the third century. We know little about the men and women who died there in the first and second centuries, but from the third century on, literary and physical evidence becomes more plentiful. With the emergence of the Church from the catacombs in the fourth century, the shrines of the Roman martyrs became sites of pilgrimage, with churches erected over their tombs to accommodate the faithful. In the middle of the fourth century, Constantine established his new capital on the Bosporus, and the imperial program to honor the martyrs shifted from Rome to Constantinople; relics of many saints were brought to "New Rome". By the end of the sixth century, when Saint Gregory the Great put the finishing touches on the Canon, his two lists of saints reflected both the illustrious history of the early Roman martyrs and the devotion of the Roman people to other saints who inspired them.

In this essay I rely primarily on *The Saints of the Canon of the Mass* by V. L. Kennedy.[1] Father Kennedy brings together much scholarly research written in German or French, and although the work is fifty years old, it has not to my knowledge been superseded. A wealth of legends surrounds the early saints, and Kennedy explains that in attempting to discern the underlying history, scholars examine three kinds of evidence: monumental (tombs, inscriptions, buildings, art), liturgical (martyrologies [calendar lists of saints] and sacramentaries), and literary (acts, passions, and legends). "Acts" relate the interrogation of the accused parties, and court records may have been used in their composition. "Passions" are accounts of the execution of the martyrs, whose suffering and death is presented as an imitation of the Passion of Christ. The "legends" of the martyrs were composed after the end of the age of persecution and often long after the events they relate. They were written for the edification of Christians and frequently dwelt on (and magnified) the marvelous.

According to Hippolyte Delehaye, a pioneer in the study of the genre, a legend is "a homage the Christian community pays to its patron saints".[2] Legends do not convey much

[1] V. L. Kennedy, C.S.B., *The Saints of the Canon of the Mass*, 2nd ed., rev. (1938; Rome: Pontificio Istituto di Archeologia Cristiana, 1963).

[2] Hippolyte Delehaye, S.J., *The Legends of the Saints*, trans. Donald Attwater (London: Geoffrey Chapman, 1962), p. xx. Delehaye (1859–

historical information, as we would understand the term—in the ancient world, history was related to rhetoric, and its purpose was to edify and inspire. The authors of such accounts were "the people", who shared stories and elaborated on them. We will encounter some instances where the legends of saints in another part of the world came to be attached to figures mentioned in the Roman Canon. Delehaye observes that there is no direct proportion between a saint's popularity and the historicity of stories about him. On the contrary, popular devotion has a life of its own. For example, several of the martyrs in the Canon are just names to us, but they must have been important enough in Rome at one time to merit inclusion in the Eucharistic Prayer. On the other hand, Saint Justin Martyr was one of the most significant Christian authors in Rome in the second century and the founder of an influential philosophical school; the account of his trial is a precious historical document—but he did not find a place in the universal Roman calendar until 1882.

What has been said thus far applies to early Christian saints in general; two additional points should be made concerning Rome itself that have a bearing on the veneration of the martyrs there. First, as the capital of the empire, the city by the Tiber had a very international population; there were residents from all over the known world, and a good many popes were Greek, Syrian, or African by birth or nationality. Devotion to a certain saint passed from a particular ethnic group to the broader populace very readily. (This is true

---

1941) devoted his life to hagiographical studies. He belonged to the Bollandists, a group of Jesuit scholars that has edited the *Acta Sanctorum* since the seventeenth century. *Legends of the Saints* was first published in 1905; a revised edition appeared in 1927.

today as well. A couple of years ago, I was surprised on a visit to Mexico City to find shrines in many churches to Saint Sharbel, a Lebanese monk who died in 1898 and was canonized in 1977. There is a sizeable Lebanese community in Mexico, and in the past thirty years devotion to this Maronite monk has spread into the wider Mexican population.) Several saints mentioned in the Canon are "imports" from other places. The second significant factor is the existence and history of the *tituli* of Rome. The early Christians met in private homes for worship; some of these were large villas, others were tenements that had been converted to Christian use. On the walls of ancient Roman buildings, a marble plaque, called a *titulus*, was engraved with the name of the building's owner. When Christianity emerged from the catacombs, there were twenty-five of these *tituli* in the city functioning as community centers. Churches were built on many of these sites in succeeding centuries. But another transformation took place as well: the name of the original owner of the building sometimes became associated with a saint of the same name; so, for instance, the *titulus Clementis* eventually became the *titulus Sancti Clementis*. As Delehaye observes, ideas may come and go, but pictures remain, and there is a human instinct to attach memories to specific places—the locale becomes the carrier of the story.

In the pages that follow we will explore the devotion to the saints mentioned in the Canon from the fourth to the sixth centuries, the period in which the Eucharistic Prayer was taking shape. We know that the lists changed somewhat over time and that there was some variation between the saints mentioned in Rome and those honored in other cities such as Milan or Ravenna. We must also bear in mind this sober warning: "As a general rule, it can be said that the historical information to be extracted from the passions or legends of the Saints, whose names are found in the Canon, is remarkably small. With the exception of the Acts and Passion of Saint Cyprian and the Passion of Saint Felicity, we must class the remainder of the legends of the saints of the Canon with what Father Delehaye calls the historical romances."[3] This may sound disconcerting at first, almost as if Kennedy were saying, "We really know very little, and most of that is not true." I think such a conclusion would be misguided for two reasons. First, the names mentioned in the Canon conjure up the whole era of witness to the Gospel under the horrible conditions that prevailed during the first several centuries of the Church's life; the names are for the most part common enough, so we can be fairly sure that people bearing those names did lay down their lives for their faith. More importantly, it was not just one or another heroic figure who handed on the faith, but the whole community of believers, many of whom—then as in our own era—suffered anonymously, their particular story never being recorded. We can see these particular women and men as representative of the martyrs of every age. Secondly, the Roman Canon also reflects the faith of believers from the fourth through the sixth centuries—what qualities they admired, what virtues they celebrated. The stories of the saints they loved embodied those virtues and have much to teach us. In the words of Father Delehaye, "It is impossible for the people's mind to be strongly impressed by some great event or by some powerful personality without their feelings finding expression in stories in which popular fancy is given full play."[4]

[3] Kennedy, *The Saints of the Canon of the Mass*, p. 94.
[4] Delehaye, *Legends of the Saints*, pp. xix–xx.

I. The Memento of the Living

The first list of saints in the Roman Canon was organized by Gregory the Great in two sets of twelve names, totaling twenty-four, a number reminiscent of the twenty-four elders in the Book of Revelation. The first set consists of the twelve Apostles, with Saint Paul taking the place of Saint Matthias; the second set is made up of twelve early martyrs, arranged in hierarchical order: bishops, other clergy, laymen. The group of twenty-four is led by the Blessed Virgin Mary (accompanied, since 1962, by Saint Joseph).

The Blessed Virgin Mary

Although there are countless churches and shrines today dedicated to the Mother of God in Rome, her liturgical cult in this city began relatively late—the first feast seems to have been a celebration in her honor on the octave day of Christmas, January 1, established sometime in the sixth century. This is not to say that there was no devotion to her: her frequent portrayal in the art of the catacombs and references to her in the preaching of the early Fathers suggests that Mary has always been venerated by the Roman people.

A great impetus was given to the veneration of our Lady by the controversy surrounding a popular title given to her in the East, the *Theotokos*, and the defense of this title at the Council of Ephesus in 431. The issue at stake was not primarily Mary, but her Son's identity: because he is truly the eternal Son of God, the second Person of the Trinity, who received in time a human nature from his mother, it is fitting to address her as "Mother of God". In the wake of the council, devotion to Mary grew considerably; for example, the church of Saint Mary Major in Rome was enlarged and decorated with mosaics and stands today as a visual monument to the teaching of Ephesus. The mosaics in the arch over the altar celebrate Christ as the Savior of Jews and Gentiles and commemorate Mary as the ever-Virgin Mother of God.

It was probably at the same time (mid-fifth century) that the name of Mary was placed in the Canon or, if it was already there, expanded to reflect the teaching of the ecumenical council. She is honored with special reverence among the saints (*in primis*) and described in terms of two dogmatic teachings of the first centuries: ever-Virgin and Mother of God. Mary's perpetual virginity was presumed or explicitly preached by several eminent Fathers, most importantly in the West by Saint Ambrose. Concerning her divine maternity, the wording of the prayer in the Canon marries the language of East and West: she is *[Mater] Dómini nostri Iesu Christi*, "Mother of our Lord Jesus Christ", and *Theotokos*, *Genetrícis Dei*.[5]

The liturgical veneration of Mary continued to grow in Rome, initially enriched by the adoption of feasts held in her honor in the East. Sometime in the seventh century, the January 1 celebration of Mary, the Mother of God, was augmented by four feasts commemorating her birth

---

[5] The term *Theotokos* literally means "she who gave birth to the one who is God". The most precise Latin rendition is *Deipara* ("Birth-giver of God"); another variation (used in the Canon) is *Dei Genetrix* ("God-bearer"). The Western Fathers were anxious to avoid confusion with the pagan cults of "mother goddess", and for this reason they initially did not translate *Theotokos* as *Mater Dei* ("Mother of God"). This term became common only when the orthodox understanding of Mary's divine maternity was firmly established.

(September 8), the Annunciation (March 25), her Purification (February 2), and Assumption (August 15). Pope Sergius I (687–701), of Syrian background, added greater solemnity to these four feasts with solemn processions from the church of Saint Hadrian in the Forum (formerly the Senate House) to the church of Saint Mary Major.

Saint Joseph

The addition of the name of Saint Joseph to the Roman Canon in 1962 was the most significant change made to the prayer in many centuries. Devotion to the spouse of Mary and the foster-father of Jesus developed very gradually in the life of the Church. In part this is because in early times liturgical veneration was given only to martyrs and also because it was necessary in the first centuries to safeguard the dogma of the Incarnation: emphasis on the fact that Jesus is the Son of God, born of a virgin, placed Joseph in the background.

The Coptic Church may have celebrated a feast in honor of Saint Joseph as far back as the fifth century. The Gospel account of the flight into Egypt created among the Copts a sense of a special tie with the Holy Family, and accounts of their sojourn there were related in the early apocryphal gospels. (It is interesting to note that Joseph appears several times in the fifth-century mosaics in Saint Mary Major: the annunciation to him of Mary's virginal conception of Jesus, the presentation of the infant Christ in the Temple, and the depiction of a legend in which, when Mary and Joseph brought the newborn Savior into Egypt, the idols in that land collapsed.) The first known church in the West to be dedicated to Saint Joseph was built in Bologna in the year

1129. In the Middle Ages, Western piety emphasized the humanity of Christ, and especially his infancy and crucifixion; reflection on Jesus' childhood naturally led to greater interest in the man chosen to be his guardian. His feast on March 19 gradually became more and more popular (although why he is honored on that date is uncertain), and devotion to him was fostered by such great saints as Bernardine of Siena and Teresa of Avila.

Veneration of Saint Joseph continued to grow throughout the nineteenth century, and, in 1870, Pope Pius IX proclaimed him patron of the universal Church. Pius' successor, Leo XIII, had this to say:

> The special motives for which St. Joseph has been proclaimed Patron of the Church, and from which the Church looks for singular benefit from his patronage and protection, are that Joseph was the spouse of Mary and that he was reputed the Father of Jesus Christ. From these sources have sprung his dignity, his holiness, his glory. In truth, the dignity of the Mother of God is so lofty that naught created can rank above it. But as Joseph has been united to the Blessed Virgin by the ties of marriage, it may not be doubted that he approached nearer than any to the eminent dignity by which the Mother of God surpasses so nobly all created natures. For marriage is the most intimate of all unions which from its essence imparts a community of gifts between those that by it are joined together. Thus in giving Joseph the Blessed Virgin as spouse, God appointed him to be not only her life's companion, the witness of her maidenhood, the protector of her honor, but also, by virtue of the conjugal tie, a participator in her sublime dignity. And Joseph shines among all mankind by the most august dignity, since by divine will, he was the guardian of the Son of God and reputed as His father

among men. Hence it came about that the Word of God was humbly subject to Joseph, that He obeyed him, and that He rendered to him all those offices that children are bound to render to their parents.[6]

Joseph was viewed as a model not only for husbands and fathers, but for workers as well. The spread of communism throughout the twentieth century led to celebrations on May 1 to honor "the workers", and in 1955 Pope Pius XII established the feast of Saint Joseph the Worker on that date.

Throughout the nineteenth century, petitions arrived in Rome asking for Joseph's name to be included in the Canon of the Mass. Several hundred bishops at the First Vatican Council asked that greater liturgical honors be extended to him, and in 1887, 632 bishops (out of 900 canvassed) signed a petition requesting Pope Leo to add Joseph's name to the Canon. Requests continued to come, and, during the first session of the Second Vatican Council, several bishops made interventions to this end. On November 13, 1962, Pope John announced to the assembled bishops his decision to add Saint Joseph's name to the Roman Canon.

The Twelve Apostles

There is evidence in Rome of devotion to the Apostles as a group. They are portrayed together in the catacombs and other early art, most notably the late-fourth-century mosaic in the church of Santa Pudenziana, one of the earliest surviving Christian figural mosaics. The order given to their names in the Canon is somewhat puzzling. The twelve Apostles are listed four times in the New Testament, never in pre-

[6] Leo XIII, encyclical *Quamquam pluries*, no. 3.

cisely the same order (this is particularly intriguing in the case of the Gospel of Luke and Acts, written by the same author). The list of the Apostles in the Canon is closest to that given in Saint Matthew's Gospel, but with two significant changes: Thomas and James the Less are both placed ahead of Bartholomew. The most likely explanation is that initially only a few Apostles were named in the Canon, and Thomas and James were added when churches were built in their honor in Rome; sometime later, probably by the end of the fifth century, the complete list of Apostles was put into the prayer.[7]

PETER and PAUL: These two saints, the greatest of the Apostles and twin stars of the Church of Rome, must be treated together, for they are inseparable as recipients of devotion by the Roman people. They are the New Testament figures about whom we know the most, apart from the Savior himself. Their martyrdom in Rome is mentioned as far back as Clement (ca. 96) and Ignatius of Antioch (ca. 107), and the traditions that Peter was crucified upside down and Paul was beheaded go back to the second century. (As a Roman citizen, Paul could not be crucified.) It is generally assumed that they both perished during the first persecution of Christians under Emperor Nero.

Writing toward the end of the second century, a Roman

---

[7] Neil J. Roy, in an essay entitled "The Mother of God, the Forerunner, and the Saints of the Roman Canon: A Euchological *Deësis*", points out that after the major Apostles (Peter, Paul, Andrew, James, and John), all of the other Apostles are listed according to the order in which their feasts occur in the Roman calendar, beginning with Thomas (whose feast was formerly on December 21). Maxwell Johnson, ed., *Issues in Eucharistic Praying in East and West* (Collegeville, Minn.: Liturgical Press, 2011), p. 335.

priest named Gaius made reference to the monuments built over their graves, one on the Vatican hill and the other on the road to Ostia. After the Edict of Milan, Emperor Constantine built churches on these two sites, the predecessors of today's basilicas of Saint Peter and Saint Paul Outside-the-Walls. The authenticity of these sites is indicated by the fact that the emperor went to great trouble to erect these churches in very precise locations, places that created logistical challenges. Saint Peter's was erected on a side of a hill, and it was necessary to destroy a cemetery to build the basilica, something abhorrent to the Roman sense of the sacredness of burial grounds. Saint Paul's was built next to a very busy road connecting Rome with its seaport. It soon became apparent that this church was far too small to accommodate the large number of pilgrims. The road, however, could not be relocated, so the imaginative decision was made to reverse the orientation of the basilica; what this suggests is that the only obstacle more insuperable than the location of the road was the location of the tomb—the basilica had to enshrine one precise spot. Excavations carried out under the present-day Saint Peter's have confirmed that the church was built over a site venerated by the Christians of Rome as Peter's tomb from the second century on, and similar work at Saint Paul's today serves to confirm the tradition of the burial of the Apostle of the Gentiles there. Graffiti, inscriptions, and paintings testify to devotion to these two Apostles in Rome all through the early centuries of the Christian era.

The earliest liturgical mention is made in the *Depositio Martyrum* of 354, which speaks of a commemoration of Peter and Paul on June 29 as far back as the year 258. Along with the two tombs, the *Depositio* makes reference to a site on the Appian Way. This was a pagan cemetery, but for some reason after the year 240 graffiti honoring Peter and Paul appeared here, and around that time a large area was cleared to allow people to gather for the *refrigerium*, the Roman meal celebrated at a graveside. Along with building churches over the tombs of the Apostles, Constantine also erected a church here, known as the *Basilica Apostolorum* (later the church was associated with Saint Sebastian). Toward the end of the fourth century, Pope Damasus placed a plaque in this church stating that for a time Peter and Paul's remains had been here. Most scholars surmise that during the persecution by Valerian in the third century, the relics of the Apostles may have been moved here for a time. Although the theory is not without its problems, it is the most likely explanation for the fact that Peter and Paul were honored here for a certain period of time.

Peter and Paul had their differences in life but were united in their witness to Christ. The Roman conviction that they are inseparable is reflected in the list of the Apostles given in the Canon, since Paul is inserted into the list of the Twelve immediately after Peter.

ANDREW: Peter's brother is called by the Greeks *protocletos*, "first-called", because he introduced Peter to the Lord (Jn 1:35–42). According to tradition, he evangelized Greece and the area around the Black Sea and was crucified on an X-shaped cross. His feast on November 30 can be traced back to the beginning of the fifth century in Jerusalem. Around the year 475, Pope Simplicius (468–483) built a church in his honor on the Esquiline hill, near Saint Mary Major. Gregory the Great held him in high regard: his monastery in Rome was under the patronage of Saint Andrew. Emperor Constantine had the relics of Saint Andrew brought to

Constantinople, and he has been regarded as the patron saint of that city ever since. The crusaders carried off his relics to Amalfi in the year 1208, and from there they went to Rome in 1462. In 1964, Pope Paul VI returned them to Patriarch Athenagoras.

JAMES: This James is the son of Zebedee, brother of John, and together with his brother and Peter he enjoyed a greater intimacy with our Lord than the other Apostles did: they alone were present for the raising of the daughter of Jairus (Mk 5:37ff.), the Transfiguration (Mk 9:2–8), and the agony in the garden (Mt 26:37–46). He was the first Apostle to die a martyr's death, as is recorded in the Acts of the Apostles 12:1–3. Later legends claim he preached the Gospel in Spain; although this is questionable, the discovery of his relics there in the ninth century made his shrine in Galicia one of the most important pilgrimage sites from the Middle Ages on. His feast has been celebrated in the West on July 25 since the ninth century. There is no evidence of a particular veneration of him in Rome during the centuries when the Canon was taking shape.

JOHN: As mentioned, he was, with Peter and James, an Apostle who enjoyed a greater intimacy with Christ and is also identified with the "beloved disciple" who rested his head on Jesus at the Last Supper. He was the only Apostle present at the crucifixion. Together with Peter, he preached the Gospel in Samaria and later lived in Ephesus, where he was buried. The Gospel, three Letters, and the Book of Revelation are attributed to him. In Rome, an oratory was built in his honor in the baptistery of the basilica of Saint John Lateran in the fifth century, and his feast on December 27 was observed as far back as the sixth century. Later his name, together with that of John the Baptist, was associated with Rome's cathedral. There is a legend that he visited Rome and was immersed in boiling oil but miraculously survived; a church commemorating this event was erected in the eighth century.

THOMAS: Known also as Didymus ("the twin"), this is the Apostle who was absent when the risen Christ appeared to the others and would not believe unless he could touch the Lord's wounds (Jn 20). From the seventh century on, his feast was celebrated on December 21, but in the revision of the calendar after the Second Vatican Council, it was moved to July 3, so that it could be observed with more solemnity outside the Advent season.[8] July 3 was the date on which his relics were transferred to Edessa, and it is also the date when he is commemorated by the "Thomas Christians" in southern India, where he evangelized. In the early sixth century, an oratory was built in his honor in Saint Peter's basilica.

PHILIP and JAMES: These two saints have been honored together in Rome since the sixth century, when their relics were placed in a basilica dedicated to the Holy Apostles. Formerly their feast was on May 1, the dedication day of

[8] It might be helpful to comment briefly on the changes in the calendar of the saints following the Second Vatican Council. Two of the major principles that governed the revision were: 1. placing greater emphasis on the "temporal cycle" celebrating the life of our Lord by, when feasible, moving saints' days out of the Advent/Christmas and Lent/Easter seasons; 2. when, as is true for many early martyrs, little beyond the name of the saint was known, removing them from the universal calendar to make room for later saints about whom we know much more. This does not mean that they "lost their haloes": they are still found in the *Roman Martyrology* and may be commemorated on their feast days.

that church, but it has been moved to May 3, because of the feast of Saint Joseph the Worker. James the Less was the son of Alphaeus and a relative of Jesus; he was called "the brother of the Lord" (Gal 1:19). James was the leader of the Christian community in Jerusalem (Acts 15:13ff.) and was martyred there sometime during the first century. A letter in the New Testament is attributed to him. Philip was a native of Bethsaida who recognized Jesus as the Messiah and told Nathaniel about him (Jn 1:45); he also introduced some Greeks to Jesus (Jn 12:20–22). Tradition has it that he evangelized Scythia, the region north and northeast of the Black Sea.

BARTHOLOMEW: This Apostle is traditionally identified with Nathaniel, because Matthew's list of the Apostles links Nathaniel with Philip, who in John's Gospel told Nathaniel that Jesus was the Messiah. He was one of the first disciples of Jesus and was present at the wedding feast of Cana. From the ninth century on, his feast in the West was celebrated on either August 24 or 25, the latter date coinciding with a commemoration of the translation of his relics in the East; only in 1570 was it definitely set on August 24. There are traditions of his evangelizing many places, especially Armenia; he was flayed and then decapitated. His relics were brought to Benevento in the ninth century and, then, to Rome, where they were placed in a church on Tiber Island.

MATTHEW: Also known as Levi, he was the tax collector who left everything to follow Jesus. He was a native of Capernaum, and according to an early tradition he wrote the Gospel attributed to him in Aramaic, from which a Greek translation was made. He evangelized Ethiopia, and his relics were brought from there to Paestum and in the tenth century to Salerno. There may have been a church dedicated to him in Rome in the fifth century, and his feast has been celebrated on September 21 since the eighth century.

SIMON and JUDE: Simon was surnamed "the Zealot", and Jude was surnamed Thaddeus (Mk 3:18). Jude was the author of a short letter in the New Testament and was related to James, "the brother of the Lord". According to a sixth-century tradition, Simon and Jude evangelized Persia. There was a chapel dedicated to them in the old Saint Peter's basilica, and their relics are preserved in Saint Peter's today. Their feast on October 28 can be traced back to the tenth century.

The Twelve Martyrs

The Apostles are followed immediately by the three earliest successors of Saint Peter, as these were given in second-century lists of the Bishops of Rome.

LINUS and CLETUS: There is no evidence of any particular devotion to these saints in the early centuries, not even legends about their presumed martyrdom. Irenaeus identified Linus with a companion of Paul who sent greetings to Timothy from Rome (2 Tim 4:21). Cletus' name comes from the Greek name *Anencletus* and is sometimes rendered as "Anacletus". The name means "blameless" and was not uncommon among slaves. Because little is known about them apart from their names, Linus and Cletus were removed from the universal calendar after the Second Vatican Council; however, they continue to be listed in the *Roman Martyrology* on September 23 (Linus) and April 26 (Cletus).

CLEMENT: Unlike the two preceding pontiffs, Saint Clement was a renowned figure, and devotion to him was strong in Rome and elsewhere. Origen identifies him with the collaborator of Saint Paul (Phil 4:3), and Irenaeus writes that Clement knew the Apostles Peter and Paul and learned their doctrine. He is the author of a letter from the Church of Rome to the Church of Corinth, written around the year 95; this letter is one of the most important documents outside of the New Testament to come down to us and was even considered canonical in some Christian communities in the early centuries. The letter was occasioned by a revolt in the Corinthian Church whereby some leaders were deposed and is an early example of Roman oversight of the wider Church. Several other writings were wrongly attributed to Clement. In the late fourth century, a church in honor of the martyr Clement was built at the site of the house-church *titulus Clementis*, and while we cannot be certain that Clement did live in that location, the identification should not be lightly dismissed. (A later legend identifies him—incorrectly—with Titus Flavius Clemens, a cousin of Emperor Domitian, who was executed for "atheism" early in the second century; but it may be that Saint Clement was a freedman in his household.) The church was rebuilt and beautifully decorated in the sixth century, another testimony to the popularity of this saint in Rome. In the fifth century, a legend grew up about Clement's martyrdom: he had been exiled to Crimea and later executed by being thrown into the sea tied to an anchor. In the late nineteenth century, the area beneath the twelfth-century church of Saint Clement was excavated, and pilgrims can visit the remains of the fifth-century church and, below that, the streets and homes of first-century Rome. Since the fourth century the feast of Saint Clement has been celebrated on November 23.

SIXTUS: This is the second pope with this name, martyred during the persecution by Emperor Valerian in the year 258; Saint Cyprian gives some details of the event in a letter, so we have a contemporaneous report. (Cyprian's letter may be found in the Office of Readings for the feast of Saint Sixtus and companions, August 7.) Valerian forbade Christians to gather in cemeteries and ordered the execution of Church officials. On August 6, 258, Pope Valerian and four of his deacons were apprehended at a gathering in the cemetery of Callistus and immediately beheaded. Two other deacons were killed that same day in a different cemetery, and Lawrence was martyred a few days later. Deacons were the principal administrative officials of the Church, so the execution of the Bishop of Rome and his entire staff was a serious blow to the Christian community. The persecution was so fierce that the priests who assumed responsibility for the governance of the Church waited until Valerian's death two years later to elect a new pope. The cemetery of Callistus served as a burial ground for Christians from the beginning of the third century. One of its rooms was a papal crypt, in which all the popes from Saint Zephyrinus (d. 218) to Saint Eutychianus (d. 283) were buried. Sixtus and his four deacons were interred here, and an oratory was erected in their honor. Saint Sixtus' feast has been celebrated on August 7 (the sixth being the feast of the Transfiguration) since 258.

CORNELIUS and CYPRIAN: These two great pastors have always been honored together, and the compiler of the list of

saints in the Canon violated his general principle of following a chronological order and placed Cornelius after Sixtus, so that he could be named with Cyprian. Cornelius
was elected pope in the year 251, immediately following a
time of fierce persecution by Emperor Decius. For two years
Rome had been without a bishop, and the spokesman for
the governing clergy, one Novatian, expected to be elected.
Cornelius was chosen instead, but Novatian refused to accept this state of affairs and had himself ordained bishop by
a rival party. The Roman Church experienced a period of
schism, and one of Cornelius' stalwart defenders was the
Bishop of Carthage, Cyprian. Cornelius was arrested and
exiled to Civitavecchia, where he later died. There is a very
touching letter written from Cyprian to Cornelius in his ex-
ile, which is found in the Office of Readings on their feast
day, September 16. Although Cornelius was not executed,
he was considered a martyr because death was brought on
as a result of his sufferings. Saint Cyprian wrote of him in
a letter: "Our colleague Cornelius was a peaceable and just
priest and deemed worthy of a martyr's death by our Lord"
(Letter 67, 6). Cornelius' body was brought back to Rome
and buried in the cemetery of Callistus; his is the first papal
epitaph to be written, not in Greek, but in Latin.

Cyprian served as Bishop of Carthage for ten years, from
248 to 258. Like Cornelius, he had to contend with a fac-
tion that rejected his leadership, and both bishops had to deal
with the vexing question of how to treat Christians who had
denied their faith during persecution. Cyprian wrote trea-
tises on this question and on the unity of the Church, and his
many letters provide an invaluable window on Christian life
in the third century. In the year 258 he was arrested, tried,

and executed; the account of the trial is also in the Office of Readings for September 16.

These two great pastors have always been honored together in the calendar. Saint Jerome says that they died on the same day, but in different years; while this seems unlikely, it suggests that as far back as the end of the fourth century they shared the same feast day. Saint Leo the Great may have built a basilica in honor of Cornelius, but it does not survive. In the seventh or eighth century, the walls of Cornelius' tomb were adorned with paintings, one of which pictures Cornelius and Cyprian together.

LAWRENCE: This deacon is without doubt one of the most popular saints with the Roman people; there are at least nine historic churches bearing his name in the city. Lawrence served as deacon to Pope Sixtus II and was put to death four days after his bishop and his six fellow deacons. He was buried on the Via Tiburtina, outside the walls of the city. Constantine built a church over his tomb, which was enlarged in the following century; Pope Damasus erected a basilica in his honor within the city walls. His feast has been observed with great solemnity on August 10 ever since his death in the year 258. (It is noteworthy that he is the only non-biblical saint whose commemoration is a "feast" and not just a "memorial" in the universal Roman calendar.) Saint Ambrose is a source for the famous legend about his martyrdom: Lawrence was asked to hand over the treasures of the Church, and he presented the poor to the examining magistrate; he was then put to death on a gridiron and died joking with his torturers. Scholars doubt the historicity of this tale, because the directive given by Valerian was that

Christian clergy were to be summarily executed, and the circumstances of Lawrence's death would fit in better with the Diocletian persecution at the beginning of the fourth century. But the story certainly suggests that Lawrence was noted for his concern for the poor and his cheerfulness. As Father Delehaye observes: "All the learned societies can join together and proclaim that Saint Lawrence could not have been tortured in the way that is said; but till the end of the world the gridiron will be the only recognized emblem of that famous Roman deacon."[9]

CHRYSOGONUS: Saint Chrysogonus was a bishop martyred in Aquileia in the second or third century. How did he come to be honored in Rome? There was a church built in Rome in the fourth century on the site of an early house-church, the *titulus Chrysogoni*. Only in the sixth century did this come to be called *titulus S. Chrysogoni*, and it seems that the third-century martyr was associated with the fourth-century church sometime in the fifth century. The legend grew up that Chrysogonus was in fact a Roman cleric and the teacher of Saint Anastasia. (Her name also appears in the Canon, and we will hear about her later.) Chrysogonus was brought before Emperor Diocletian, who was in residence in Aquileia, and there condemned to death. Scholars believe that this story developed to explain the presence of two ancient places of worship, later the sites of churches (San Crisogono and Santa Anastasia) dedicated to martyrs who had not died in Rome. Although Saint Chrysogonus is no longer on the universal calendar, his name still appears in the *Roman Martyrology* on November 24.

[9] Delehaye, *Legends of the Saints*, p. xix.

Appendix: The Saints of the Roman Canon

JOHN and PAUL: The story of these two saints brings us to the dim underworld of Christian life during the era of persecution and illustrates how later legends were developed to shed light on the hidden past. To begin with the archeological evidence: early in the fifth century, a wealthy Roman noble, Pammachius, built a basilica on the Caelian Hill in Rome. (Pammachius was a well-known figure, and we have letters to him from Jerome, Augustine, and Paulinus of Nola.) This building was known as the *titulus Pammachii*. Why did he build it there? Excavations under the church have revealed that it was the site of a second-century tenement building, an edifice with shops on the ground level and apartments on the upper floors. Sometime in the middle of the third century, the ground floor of this tenement was decorated with murals, some with Christian themes; the floor above was converted into a large hall. Clearly this tenement, a nondescript building from the street, functioned as a Christian house-church during the era of persecution. Another name attached to the site is *titulus Byzantii*, so its original owner may have been one Byzantius. In the late fourth century, a small oratory with a depository for relics was built between the ground floor and the first story. This oratory was located under the altar on the floor above and was decorated with paintings of two saints and scenes of martyrdom. In the early fifth century, Pammachius tore down the upper floors of the tenement and used the remainder as the foundation for his basilica; by the end of the sixth century, the church was also known as the *titulus SS. Ioannis et Pauli*.

According to legend, Saints John and Paul were martyred under Emperor Julian the Apostate, who ordered them to be buried in their own home to prevent their being honored as martyrs. A second legend relates that a subsequent Christian emperor ordered a certain senator Byzantius to locate their bodies and build a church in their honor; yet another legend identifies Byzantius as the father of Pammachius. There are significant reasons to question the veracity of these accounts, however. There were no Christians executed in the West during the reign of Julian (and few in the East), and at that time the Roman prohibition against allowing burials in the city was still strictly enforced; no one, not even the emperor, could sanction this. It is thought that the "Passion of John and Paul" was adapted from the story of Saints Juventinus and Maximinus, Roman soldiers in the East who did suffer martyrdom under Julian.

Who, then, were John and Paul? The best hypothesis is that when the oratory was built in the tenement in the late fourth century, it received the relics of several martyrs, two of whom were named John and Paul. Their names became associated with the site, and the later legend was developed to explain who the patron saints of the basilica were and why—in contrast to all other Roman martyrs—they were not buried outside city walls. John and Paul are no longer on the universal calendar but are listed in the *Roman Martyrology* on June 26.

COSMAS and DAMIAN: These two Syrian martyrs were very popular in the East, venerated both for their heroic witness and because they were doctors who would not charge their patients. In the sixth century, Emperor Justinian erected a spacious church over their burial site in Cyr, and devotion to them spread from Constantinople to Ravenna and from there to Rome. In the early sixth century, Pope Symmachus (498–514) built an oratory in their honor in the church of Saint Mary Major. Several years later, Pope Felix IV (526–530) converted two pagan temples in the Forum into a church in their honor. The date of their feast, September 26, marks the anniversary of the dedication of that church.

II. The Memento of the Dead

In several Eastern Eucharistic Prayers, Saints John the Baptist and Stephen are mentioned in connection with the intercessory prayer for the dead, and we find the same to be true in the Roman Canon. Over time several more martyrs were added, totaling (in addition to John) seven men and seven women.

Saint John the Baptist

Josephus tells us that Herod had John the Baptist executed at his desert palace of Machaerus, east of the Dead Sea, but in the early centuries of the Christian era his remains were venerated at a church in Sebaste; Julian the Apostate had this basilica ransacked and the martyr's relics destroyed. But pilgrims continued to go there, and Saint Jerome reported miraculous healings. Relics may have survived, too, judging by the number of churches throughout the Christian world claiming to possess them. This great number of relics (authentic or not) and the countless churches dedicated to Saint John the Baptist testify to his great popularity. The oldest liturgical commemoration we have of Saint John is the feast of his nativity, June 24. This celebration may go back to the mid-fourth century in Rome, and we know that it was also a major event in Africa (a sermon by Saint Augustine for the occasion may be found in the Office of Readings for June 24). By the sixth century, this feast was being observed with a vigil and fast in Rome. Another feast, commemorating his execution, has been celebrated on August 29 since the fifth century. The *Liber Pontificalis* states that Emperor Constantine built two churches in John's honor near Rome, one at Albano and another at Ostia, but nothing survives of these. The earliest recorded place of worship in Rome itself is a chapel built in the cathedral baptistery in honor of Saint John the Baptist by Pope Hilarus (461–468) around the year 465.

Seven Male Martyrs

STEPHEN: Devotion to the deacon and proto-martyr was greatly increased when his body was discovered in the year 415. The church built in his honor in Jerusalem was one of the largest in the city; it was destroyed by the Persians in the seventh century. Stephen was particularly venerated in Africa, and from there the devotion spread to Rome. In the mid-fifth-century, a woman named Demetria built a church in his honor on the Via Latina, followed by two other major churches: Santo Stefano Rotondo on the Caelian Hill and another near the church of Saint Lawrence. In the sixth century, some of his relics were brought to Rome and placed with those of the popular deacon-martyr of Rome, Lawrence. His feast has been observed on December 26 from at least the fifth century, not only in Rome, but in Syria and Carthage as well; the *dies natalis* (birth to eternal life) of the first martyr for Christ was thereby linked to the birth of the Savior.

MATTHIAS: Little is known of the life or death of the disciple chosen to take the place of Judas among the twelve Apostles. There is no evidence of devotion to him in Rome until the ninth century, and it seems that his name was added to the Canon simply to compensate for the fact that he was removed from the list of the Twelve in the *Memento* of the living to make room for Saint Paul. His feast was observed on February 24, apparently in connection with the claims of various Roman churches to have his relics; in the recent reform of the calendar, it has been moved to May 14, which is usually late in the Easter season, so that it falls during or near the nine days between Ascension and Pentecost.

BARNABAS: The companion of Paul, and according to some ancient traditions one of the seventy disciples of Jesus, Barnabas was called an Apostle in the New Testament (Acts 4:36) and has always been accorded that dignity in the liturgy. He was a native of Cyprus, and it is commonly believed that this is where he died. There is no indication of devotion to him in Rome until the eleventh century, when his feast began to be observed on June 11 (as it was in the East) because this was the anniversary of the finding of his body. This silence is somewhat surprising because a fourth-century Greek document, translated into Latin by Rufinus of Aquileia at the beginning of the fifth century, states that he was the first to preach the Gospel in Rome.

IGNATIUS OF ANTIOCH: The second successor of Peter as leader in the Church of Antioch, this great pastor was executed in Rome around the year 107. He wrote letters to various churches, including the Church of Rome, which are among the earliest extra-biblical Christian texts we have. In the late fourth century, his relics were returned to Antioch, where Saint John Chrysostom preached the sermon on the occasion of their placement there. They came back to Rome, to the church of Saint Clement, in the seventh century, when Antioch fell to the Persians. Although he was one of the outstanding figures of the sub-apostolic age, no liturgical books in the West indicate a feast for him in the early centuries. His feast was formerly celebrated on February 1 but has been moved to October 17, the date on which it has traditionally been celebrated in the Syrian calendar.

ALEXANDER: The identity of this saint is a puzzle because there were several martyrs named Alexander venerated in Rome. A fourth-century martyrology lists three groups of martyrs that include an Alexander; later liturgical books indicate feasts for two of these: on May 3, a group of martyrs on the Via Nomentana; on July 10, seven martyrs, also including an Alexander. A sixth-century legend identifies the martyr named in the first group with Pope Alexander (109–116), but this is questionable for many reasons: the tomb of these martyrs was found in the nineteenth century, and the inscriptions do not suggest that this Alexander was a bishop; Irenaeus says nothing about the martyrdom of this pope, but he does speak of the execution of his successor, Telesphorus; had the author of the list in the Canon thought that this martyr was a pope, he would have listed him before Ignatius of Antioch. It is more likely that the Alexander named here is one of the seven martyrs commemorated on July 10. Earlier documents do not suggest any relationship between these martyrs, but later legends describe them as seven brothers, sons of a woman named Felicity. In the current *Roman Martyrology* we find the following entries: May 3: "Via Nomentana, seventh mile from the city of Rome, saints Eventius, Alexander, and Theodolus, martyrs." On July 10: "At Rome, the holy martyrs Felix and Philip in the cemetery of Priscilla; Vitalis, Martialis, and Alexander in the cemetery of the *Iordani*; Silanus in the cemetery of Maximus; and Ianuarius in the cemetery of Praetextatus."

MARCELLINUS and PETER: In the inscription he placed above their tombs, Pope Damasus stated that he had heard a description of their martyrdom from the executioner himself, so it is likely that these two saints died during Diocletian's persecution in the early fourth century. They were buried on the Via Labicana, at a place known as "*ad duas lauros*" (at the two laurels). This was near the site chosen by Helena, the mother of the emperor Constantine, for her mausoleum, and she or her son built a church over the tomb of the two martyrs which was later destroyed. The crypt of this basilica was excavated in the late nineteenth century, and the resting place of the martyrs was located, although their relics had been taken to Germany in the ninth century. Their names became associated in the sixth century with a church inside the walls of Rome, on the Via Merulana. Their legend, composed at the beginning of the sixth century, describes Marcellinus as a priest and Peter as an exorcist.

Seven Female Martyrs

FELICITY and PERPETUA: The identity of these martyrs is not as straightforward as it initially appears. One of the most precious testimonies from the era of the martyrs is the *Passion of Perpetua and Felicity*, which is a contemporary account of the martyrdom of three catechumens, Saturus, Saturninus, and Revocatus, and two young women: Vibia Perpetua, twenty-two years of age and the mother of an infant son, and her slave Felicity, who was pregnant at the time of her arrest and gave birth to a baby girl while in prison. They

189

were all executed on March 7, 202, at Carthage. Much of the *Passion* is Perpetua's own diary, and two other chapters were written by Saturus. The two women are listed together in the fourth-century Roman martyrology, so it would seem that the two women mentioned in the Canon are the African martyrs, and they might well be. However, there are reasons to question whether there was a devotion to these saints in Rome in the first six centuries: there is no document or monument (chapel, oratory) dedicated to them, and in some versions of the Canon their names are not together. Also, their feast falls in March, and during the first six centuries no saints' days were celebrated in Rome during Lent. Then there is the fact that the Canon mentions Felicity first, whereas she has a secondary role in the story of the *Passion*. This suggests the strong possibility that the Canon is referring to a Roman saint named Felicity.

From the end of the fourth century, we have evidence that a martyr named Felicity was honored on the Via Salaria. Pope Boniface I (418–422) resided there while the outcome of his contested election was decided, and he expressed his gratitude by building an oratory over the saint's tomb. Nearby was the tomb of Silanus, one of the seven martyrs (including Alexander) about whom we read above. The proximity of their tombs may have given birth to the sixth-century legend that the seven martyrs were brothers and that Felicity was their mother; a sermon preached by Gregory the Great indicates that by his time the veracity of this story was assumed. Judging by the amount of evidence of veneration of this martyr, Felicity of Rome may well be the woman referred to in the Canon; and Perpetua could have been added later, with the further connection that the Roman saint had the same name as Perpetua's companion

in martyrdom. Saint Felicity of Rome is still listed in the
Roman Martyrology, on November 23.

On the other hand, we find that in the sixth-century mosaics of Ravenna, the two African saints are always represented together, and there is no trace of Felicity of Rome. If in fact the Canon refers to Perpetua and her servant, it is possible that Pope Gelasius (492–496) added their names, since he was of African origin. This latter hypothesis also harmonizes with a geographical grouping of the female martyrs: Africa (Perpetua and Felicity), Sicily (Agatha and Lucy), Rome (Agnes and Cecilia), the East (Anastasia).

Agatha and Lucy: These two women were Sicilian martyrs. Agatha was executed in Catania around the year 250, and her feast has been observed on February 5 since at least the middle of the fourth century. At the beginning of the sixth century, Pope Symmachus (598–614) built a basilica in her honor on the Via Aurelia. Saint Gregory the Great reconsecrated in her honor a church that had been built in Rome for the Arian Goths in the fifth century. He also founded a monastery in Sicily in honor of Saints Maximin and Agatha and ordered the construction of a church over her tomb in Catania. Lucy was martyred in Syracuse, probably in the persecution by Diocletian at the beginning of the fourth century. The first church honoring her in Rome was built in the mid-seventh century, and there is mention of an abbot of a monastery of Saints Andrew and Lucy in Rome in the year 600. This was during the pontificate of Gregory, who was also interested in a monastery dedicated to Saint Lucy in Syracuse. Many of this pope's letters deal with Sicily, so it is probable that it was he who encouraged devotion to these martyrs in Rome. An early eighth-century English bishop, who had been educated at the monastery school of Canterbury and visited Rome, claims that it was Gregory the Great who placed their names in the Roman Canon.

AGNES: Without a doubt, Agnes is the most popular of woman martyrs; girl martyrs, actually, because she was only twelve or thirteen when she died. She was the subject of writings by several fourth-century figures, including Damasus, Ambrose, and Prudentius. Emperor Constantine's daughter Constantia had a church built over her tomb on the Via Nomentana and placed her own mausoleum nearby. This church was enlarged in succeeding centuries, and several churches were built in her honor in the city of Rome, the most famous being the one on the Piazza Navona, traditionally identified as the place of her martyrdom. Although the details of her martyrdom vary, we can be certain that she was very young, that she was buried on the Via Nomentana, and that her feast has been celebrated on January 21 since the middle of the fourth century. There is a beautiful custom, still observed, whereby two lambs are blessed in her church on the feast of Saint Agnes, and the wool is used to make the palliums (small woolen stoles) that are then placed before the tomb of Saint Peter and bestowed each year on the feast of Saints Peter and Paul by the pope to residential archbishops, as a sign of their bond in the pastoral ministry.

CECILIA: Father Delehaye, who devoted his life to the study of the saints' legends, considered the case of this popular saint to be the most tangled question in Roman hagiography. Devotion to Cecilia emerged seemingly out of nowhere in fifth-century Rome and spread very quickly; she even appears in mosaics of female saints in Ravenna. There are two sites associated with her name. First, there is a chapel near the papal crypt in the catacomb of Callistus built for a woman named Cecilia, presumably a martyr, although there is no specific indication of this. This chapel was constructed after the era of persecution and, in the fifth century, decorated with a fresco of Saint Cecilia. Second, there is a basilica in Trastevere, built over the remains of several buildings from ancient Rome, including a mansion and baths; this was known as the *titulus Caeciliae*. The fifth-century Passion wove these two sites together. It relates that Cecilia was a noblewoman and a Christian who had taken a vow of virginity. Her parents arranged for her to marry a pagan named Valerian; Cecilia convinced him to respect her vow, and he and his brother Tiburtius became Christians. They were subsequently arrested, and Cecilia was condemned to death by suffocation in the bath at her residence. When this failed, she was beheaded. Delehaye suggests that the person associated with the site in Trastevere was a wealthy woman who had donated her property to the Church (hence, *titulus Caeciliae*) and that with the passage of time she came to be associated with the saint buried in the cemetery of Callistus. To add to the mystery, although the chapel in the catacomb was dedicated to Saint Cecilia, her remains were not found there. In the ninth century, when Pope Paschal I (817–824) rebuilt the church of Saint Cecilia in Trastevere, he found her body in the catacomb of Praetextatus, across the Appian Way from the catacomb of Callistus. This was also where the early martyrs Valerian and Tiburtius had been buried; the body that Paschal found was incorrupt, still dressed in splendid robes. Cecilia's feast day has been observed on November 22 since the fifth century.

ANASTASIA: The devotion to this woman, martyred in Sirmium (modern-day Serbia) probably during the persecution of Diocletian, is due in part to a name association with a Roman *titulus* and in part to the political situation of Rome in the sixth century. On the west side of the Palatine Hill (the site of imperial palaces and homes of the wealthy), there was a church built in the late fourth or early fifth century by a woman named Anastasia; this was known as the *titulus Anastasiae*. In the late fifth century, the body of the martyr Anastasia of Sirmium was brought to Constantinople and placed in the church of the *Anastasis* ("Resurrection"), a copy of the shrine built over the empty tomb of Jesus in Jerusalem. Devotion to this saint spread to Rome from Constantinople in the sixth century, in part because Emperor Justinian sent his great general Belisarius to expel the Goths from the western empire. Belisarius lived in Rome, and the sense of communion between "Old Rome" and "New Rome" found expression in shared devotion to the early martyrs. The *titulus Anastasiae* became the church of Saint Anastasia. Here was a church in the heart of imperial Rome dedicated, it was presumed, to the martyr of Sirmium. So, the legend developed that Anastasia had been a noblewoman, the daughter of one Praetextatus, and that Chrysogonus had been her teacher. Chrysogonus was brought before the emperor in Aquileia and condemned to death. Anastasia tended to prisoners there, then moved eastward, where she herself was martyred. The legend explained how there came to be two churches in Rome dedicated to martyrs who had in fact died in distant cities. It also celebrated the bond of faith between Rome and the imperial capital; and, for good measure, it connected the memory of a woman martyr highly venerated in Constantinople with the very heart of pagan imperial Rome. The church of Saint Anastasia in Rome was very prestigious, listed in the eighth century as third only to the cathedral and Saint Peter's; and it was customary in the Middle Ages for the pope to celebrate Mass there on the morning of December 25, its patron's feast day.

Conclusion

Clearly, the saints in the Roman Canon were organized in a deliberate pattern: two lists of 12 + 12 and 7 + 7 martyrs, arranged in hierarchical order (the men) or geographical provenance (the women). It seems likely that the final redactor was Saint Gregory the Great. Just as each of the figures had his or her historical identity and, then, attracted stories or legends in later eras, so the lists themselves developed over time, reflecting the changing fortunes of devotion to various saints from the fourth to sixth centuries. At the end of his study, Kennedy examines the lists through two lenses: geographical and chronological. These help us gain some appreciation for the organic nature of the catalogue of saints as they have come down to us. His conclusions must of necessity be hypothetical, since we know little about the life of the Roman Church during the centuries of persecution, and even in subsequent centuries we are relying on guesses drawn from the monumental and liturgical sources that have survived. These conclusions help to flesh out how Gregory's list came to be.

First, the geographical divisions. The saints whose cult was native to Rome are:

Peter, Paul, Linus, Cletus, Clement, Sixtus, Cornelius, Lawrence, Alexander, Marcellinus and Peter, Felicity [if the Roman saint], Agnes.

Non-Roman saints are:

The other Apostles, Cyprian, Chrysogonus, John and Paul, Cosmas and Damian, John the Baptist, Stephen, Matthias, Barnabas, Ignatius, Perpetua, Anastasia, Agatha, Lucy, Felicity [if this is Perpetua's servant]. John and Paul, Chrysogonus, and Anastasia are "honorary" Romans because later legends connected them with Rome.

Next Kennedy offers the following schema to suggest how devotion to various saints grew during the centuries when the Canon was taking shape.

250–384: The *terminus ad quem* is the pontificate of Damasus I (366–384), because he was assiduous in his devotion to the martyrs and erected commemorative plaques at their shrines. From these we know which saints were being honored in Rome toward the end of the fourth century.

Peter, Paul, Sixtus, Cornelius, Cyprian, Lawrence, Alexander, Marcellinus and Peter, Perpetua [and Felicity, if Perpetua's servant].

384–496: The *terminus ad quem* here is the pontificate of Gelasius I (492–496), because Gelasius had a hand in organizing the Roman liturgical books; in fact, he may have added the intercessions for the living and the dead to the Canon, with an accompanying list of some saints.

Andrew, John the Evangelist, Clement, John the Baptist, Stephen, Felicity [of Rome], Cecilia.

496–604: The *terminus ad quem* here is the pontificate of Gregory the Great (590–604), who completed the catalogue of saints in the Roman Canon.

> Thomas, Matthew [?], James and Philip, John and Paul, Cosmas and Damian, Agatha, Lucy, Anastasia.

Finally, Kennedy lists saints for whom there is no evidence of explicit veneration in Rome during the first six centuries (that is, no churches or chapels in their honor or mention in liturgical books and calendars):

> James the elder, Bartholomew, Matthew [?], Simon, Jude, Linus, Cletus, Matthias, Barnabas, Ignatius of Antioch.

Kennedy puts a question mark next to the Apostle Matthew because a priest attending a Roman synod in 499 signed himself as being from the *titulus [S.] Matthei,* so there *may* have been a church dedicated to this Apostle in Rome at the time, but it does not appear in a subsequent list a century later.

One resource that sheds light on the development of the list of saints in the Roman Canon is the liturgical texts of other places, notably Milan and Ravenna. These Eucharistic Prayers have many, but not all, of the saints found in the Roman Canon, and they add saints of their own. When the Roman Mass was adopted in France in the early Middle Ages, dioceses and communities also felt free to augment Gregory's list with some local saints. Under the reforms of Charlemagne this practice was discontinued, and the list as contained in Gregory's Canon became normative from that time on.